THE
CIRCLE
of
PROFIT

ANIK SINGAL

VSSMind Media, Inc.
8222 Flower Hill Way Unit # 273, Gaithersburg, MD 20879-4546

First Edition

ISBN-13: 978-1508458661
ISBN-10: 1508458669
www.profitacademy.com

What You're About To Master

It really does not matter if you have ever even considered being in business for yourself. It does not matter if you have any experience. All that matters is that you are not currently happy with your career or financial position. If you want more from your life, if you want a life full of financial freedom, then this is the book for you.

The author, Anik Singal is about to take you through a jaw-dropping journey that has taken him over 10 years. He started with nothing but a big dream in college and stumbled his way into the world of being an Online Entrepreneur. He had no technical knowledge, no experience and absolutely no idea what he was doing.

However, he soon became addicted to the idea of creating wealth using the Internet. That's what this book is all about. Anik Singal has dedicated his life to learning how someone can wake up every morning and go to sleep every night having done nothing but what they're passionate about. However, everyone knows, it's not enough to just live your passion; you need to create a living with it too.

The Circle of Profit is a business system that allows anyone in the World to quickly build a business empire right from their laptop. You can begin to generate millions of dollars by simply giving away information. You're about to learn how to take a topic you're passionate about, share it with everyone in the World, all while creating millions of dollars.

If you've ever dreamed of having more from your life, The Circle of Profit is just the system to get you there!

About The Author - Anik Singal

Anik Singal started his online business over 10 years ago right from his dorm room. He had absolutely no experience and stumbled into this world by mistake. After struggling for 18 months, he was just about to give up when he finally broke the first part of the code!

Within just a few years, he had built a $10 Million a year business that was operating around the world, all from the comfort of his laptop. His journey wasn't easy though. He had many ups and downs. He made millions and also lost millions. Through his journey, he has mastered the system that has gone on to change thousands of lives around the World.

Since he started teaching this system, Anik Singal has been featured in BusinessWeek as a Top 3 Entrepreneur Under 25. He has also had his Internet Business featured as an Inc 500 company for two years in a row, all using the same business systems he teaches now.

Anik Singal has spoken as a motivational and Entrepreneurship coach in front of thousands of people on stages from Singapore to London to Washington, DC. He has influenced the lives of countless thousands by sharing his one simple system that is responsible for all his success.

In his career, Anik Singal has sold over $70 Million worth of products online, all by just using his computer and a business system that he now teaches inside his Profit Academy program. It all begins with The Circle of Profit. It all begins with this.

Anik Singal has made it his personal mission now to teach his secrets to Entrepreneurs around the world looking for true financial freedom.

STOP!

A FREE Invitation That Will Change Your Life
FREE Profit Workshop – Online Classes
(Value ~~$1,497~~ – FREE)

I am very committed to your success. I really want you to have everything you need to succeed in your online business. To help you further, I have invested a lot of money to bring you some amazing free training that's worth at least $1,497.

It's called the **Profit Workshop**.

I'm hosting three LIVE training sessions. I have gone to many extremes to bring this training to your doorstep. I will be using every presentation tool at my disposal to dissect the entire Profit Academy system for you!

If you want to start generating profits online as fast as possible, please make sure to register for this Free training immediately. I have no idea how long it will be available, so take advantage right away!

I will also be introducing you to some of our most successful students who have used every piece of the Profit Academy training to become runaway successes. They will be available to answer your questions and give you everything you need.

GOAL: How To Turn Your Passions Into $1 Million
February 23rd – 8:00 p.m. Eastern
Profit Workshop #1 – How to Quickly Generate $100,000 With a Tiny System
February 26th – 8:00 p.m. Eastern
Profit Workshop #2 – How to Turn That $100,000 Into $500,000 in an Instant

March 3rd – 8:00 p.m. Eastern

Profit Workshop #3 – The Final Secret to $1 Million

Remember, if you have already missed the LIVE training date and time, it's no problem. For now, I am still making the replay available to watch. However, it can come down at any time. Take advantage right away and register for your Free training!

Save Your Free Seat Here:
www.FreeProfitWorkshop.com

Dedicated to my family and friends for all their support, love, and care.

My success is all because of you.

Contents

Section 5: Your Final Steps to $1 Million

Section 1

Your Passion, Your Life

Chapter 1
My Story

"Light yourself on fire with passion and people will come from miles to watch you." - John Wesley

In the coming pages, you're going to discover the system that will completely change your life. It's a simple circle, but when you master it, your dream life is at your fingertips.

I know that sounds a bit hard to believe. Trust me: I have lived my life bombarded with crazy claim after crazy claim. I've heard it all in my 13 years as an online entrepreneur; however, what you're reading now is not hype or exaggeration. It's a true story with a detailed system that has worked for me and my students. All I ask is that you take in every word, take the training seriously, and then execute!

My goal is to teach you a system that will allow you to live a life immersed in your passion. If you apply the teachings you read about here, you will leap out of bed every morning ready to attack the day. The moment you picked up this book, you empowered yourself with possibly the greatest-kept secret to pure financial freedom.

What you're about to get your hands on is simple and fast. It is a powerful circle that represents a system that can lead to a very profitable and fulfilling **passion business**.

A **passion business** is a lifestyle business based on your generating millions in profit simply by teaching, educating, and immersing yourself in almost any topic of your choice. Simply put, think about what makes your heart leap. It can be a hobby, a skill, or even a professional trade. Your passions can range from video games to golf to hitting the gym. If you have even a hint of knowledge on a topic that interests you, you can build a million-dollar business in almost no time. The key is just having the right system, or in this case, *the right circle*.

I'm going to show you how to use the power of the Internet to do a few things—all in an automated fashion that requires zero technical expertise:

1. Find others who share your passion on any topic.
2. Create relationships with them.
3. Begin to generate thousands (or even millions) of dollars by simply helping these people.

The truth is that the sky is the limit. I've chosen to use **The Circle of Profit** to build a company now making more than $10 million a year in sales. I have students who are earning millions and others who are happy making a few hundred thousand dollars. The Circle works the same for all levels of income.

The beauty of The Circle is that it allows you to build your business around your life. How big the circle grows is completely up to you.

Jimmy's Story

Throughout my business life and travels, I meet all kinds of people who share their stories with me. This is a personal one about a friend of mine named Jimmy.

I met Jimmy years ago and watched him slave away at his job. He was in the car business and very successful at it! He started in the business by washing cars and climbed his way to the highest management levels. However, all that success came at a steep price. I used to watch Jimmy work 16 hour days, over and over.

At the same time, Jimmy used to watch me live my life. I traveled the world. I loved my life. I lived the dream life, as he said.

One day, he had finally had enough.

He came to me and flat-out asked me to show him what I was doing. I told him if he was dead serious, I would reveal my system to him. What I shared with him was exactly what I am sharing with you in this book. As a matter of fact, I only taught him a part of what I'm teaching you.

Within just two weeks, Jimmy started to make money online.

Within a few months, Jimmy was making $3,000 to $4,000 a month, all while working super part-time. The more his eyes opened, he started to get more serious about The Circle of Profit. Within six months, Jimmy was already earning $10,000 to $15,000 a month consistently.

Finally, Jimmy quit his job. This was the day his business really took off.

The first year after quitting his job, Jimmy earned close to $250,000. His second year he was set to clear over $1 Million. His third year, he generated over $2 Million in pure profit! This year, he is estimating that he will earn over $4 Million.

Can you believe it? The best part is that he wakes up every morning fully immersed in his passion. He absolutely loves his life and his career now. He works half as hard and earns more in one year than he would have in twenty!

You see, The Circle of Profit is designed in such a way that you can get whatever you want from it. You can coast along part-time and easily earn six-figures. You can also get serious about it and start clearing multiple seven-figures. There is no right or wrong answer. The decision is completely up to you.

Your Golden Ticket

Hi, I'm Anik Singal. For more than 13 years, I've been an online entrepreneur. I've built more than a dozen Internet-based companies. I've had some become raging successes and I've even had some catastrophic failures. I've seen a lot and learned even more. **The Circle of Profit** is a result of countless wins and even more mistakes.

I'm not the only one who has profited from the Circle of Profit. I (and my team of trainers) have helped thousands of people just like you from all around the world start their own **passion businesses** with nothing more than a computer.

I've been featured in *BusinessWeek* magazine as a "Top 3 Entrepreneur Under 25" and have been featured multiple times as an *Inc 500* company. The very strategies from the Circle of Profit have won me awards around the world. I've done nothing more and nothing less than what I'm about to share with you now.

I believe in a few simple things when building a wildly successful and profitable digital business from your home:

1.   Find others among the billions of people on the Internet others who share your passion.
2.   Provide them great value using automated tools.
3.   Build an incredible relationship with them.
4.   Profit the entire time.

As you'll see in this book, there's no reason the "secrets" contained here cannot work for you. It doesn't matter if you're not "tech savvy." It doesn't matter if you don't know a line of HTML. It doesn't matter if you barely even know what a website is. The Circle of Profit is built around only information and nothing more. Everything "technical" is a matter of some automated tools that we hand right to you as a student of the **Profit Academy**.

In this business, you'll never need to raise venture capital. You'll never need to scratch at the doors of your bank praying for a loan. You just copy and paste a simple system and let it grow at any pace that you're comfortable with.

Whether you start it part-time or full-time makes no

difference. Remember, this is a system meant to fuel your passion and build the life of your dreams. Putting that very life at risk to build the business is not something I believe in, no matter how big a digital business we want to build.

If you can give me an hour a day of your time, you have what it takes.

All you need to do is read this book, understand this simple system, and most important of all, take action. I'm confident the system will work for you. I've seen The Circle of Profit transform thousands of lives right before my eyes.

Many people make the mistake of thinking that they have to be world-renowned experts or technical geniuses to build an online business. Many more make the mistake of thinking that they need to have fancy business degrees. Before you and I can dive into the Circle of Profit, it's really important that we throw these false beliefs into the dustbin.

The best way we can do that is if I tell you my own story. You'll see that I was the least likely candidate to become a successful online entrepreneur. However, as fate would have it, I was most blessed to uncover this business model and even more blessed to be able to bring it to your doorsteps today.

FREE Profit Training *($1,497 Value)*

What if you had the opportunity to learn the quickest and easiest way to start making money online while having a voice to thousands around the world? What if you were literally handed the EXACT model that thousands have used to turn their own passion into $1 Million (*or more*)?

It all starts with a simple system that will help you make your first $1 online faster than you ever imagined.

I've put together a very special series of Free training for you. This is training where I will stand in front of a white board and teach you personally. I even get my top students from around the World to show you their entire business!

The information I help you master has taken me over 10 years to perfect. You can have it in just a few hours!

I want to personally invite you to a Free training series I'm doing called the "Free Profit Workshop." There is absolutely no catch and no credit card required. You can register for it right away with just your Email address.

Just go to www.FreeProfitWorkshop.com and you will fast be on your way to turning your passion into $1 Million!

WARNING: Space in this training is very limited. This event is 100% Free but only for a limited time. In case you have missed the LIVE training sessions, we are going to make the replays available for a short time.

Whatever you do, don't miss it. Save your Free seat now!

www.FreeProfitWorkshop.com

A Dream Almost Forgotten

I grew up in a traditional Indian family where education and professional careers were always the end goal. I was surrounded by incredibly successful engineers, doctors, and lawyers. My own father is a very successful engineer to whom I owe every ounce of my success. Given the environment I grew up in, I had only one dream: I wanted to become a doctor.

I didn't have a strong basis for this dream. It was just that while growing up, I always saw how my family spoke with pride over anyone who became a doctor. I knew that doctors lived wealthy lives and were surrounded by respect from the community. Based on what I observed, for more than 18 years of my life, if anyone asked me, "Anik, what do you want to be when you grow up?" my answer was short and sweet: "Doctor."

School never came easy to me, but I was always a hard worker. I lived by the mantra of making myself and those around me proud of me. If I had to stay up all night studying, I did. If I had to step out of my comfort zone, I did.

My parents had instilled one strong teaching in me: Work hard, never quit, and achieve your dreams.

Using just those simple teachings, I worked my way through school. Having immigrated to the U.S. in the third grade, barely capable of speaking English, I burned the midnight oil all the way to the top of my high school class.

I worked my way into one of the top pre-medical programs in the world. As far as I knew, my dream was just a reach away; I was well on my path. The heavy lifting was almost over. I was in such a highly regarded pre-med program that I was virtually guaranteed admission into any top medical school.

However, with all my dreams so close, I found it shocking that I consistently felt a big empty space in my heart. Every night, I fell asleep staring at the ceiling. Every morning, I struggled to climb out of bed, tortured by the thought of going to another biology class.

As months passed, the feeling grew stronger. One day it grew so strong that I had no choice but to sit down, close the door, and force myself to consider why. I promised myself that I would not leave the room until I discovered the true reason behind my troubled heart.

That night, I did.

I kept reflecting back years before and seeing one passion I had somehow ignored. Ever since I was a child, I was mesmerized by creation. I was never the kind to simply follow orders or to do things the way everyone else did them.

My True Dream:
To create my own path. To be my own boss. To be an entrepreneur.

* * *

I was that kid in the neighborhood who set up a lemonade stand. I didn't just set-up the stand; I hired younger kids to run the stand while I sat inside watching cartoons. I was the kid who scoffed at being told what I couldn't do and rejoiced in my ability to prove them wrong.

Lost in the dream of impressing everyone around me, I had forgotten my true dream. I wanted to create. I wanted to build. I wanted to be the one in control.

As far back as I could remember, I used to make a very bold statement to all my friends. I used to say, "I'll be making over $10,000 a month by the time I graduate from college." I didn't just say this once or twice; I repeated it often.

I was consistently laughed at. I was ridiculed. I was questioned. However, it never mattered to me. I never knew *how* I was going to do it; I just knew that I would.

Well, that night I realized that becoming a doctor didn't fit my dream. Don't get me wrong; I have immense respect for doctors. They've literally saved my life countless times. However, that didn't mean that it was the right profession for me.

That same night I came to a very disturbing realization: I was going to have to change my path. I was going to have to leave this amazing pre-med program that made my parents shine with pride. I was going to venture out into the world of business where I had no guidance, no mentorship, and absolutely no resources. After struggling for months with the fear of disappointing my family, I had reached a critical juncture.

The Moment of Truth

I went to my parents in great fear. I had to share with them my plans to drop this perfect life I had built only to go into a life full of sharks and monsters. Much to my surprise yet great relief, that was the day I discovered just how amazing my parents were. They both blessed my decision and reinforced to me that my life and my dreams were mine and mine alone.

I had just won the first major battle towards a life of my dreams, but I knew that it was just beginning. The hard part was still ahead.

What was I going to do now?

I had two years to make good on my public declaration. I had two years to dive into a world I knew nothing about. I had two years to fulfill my mission of making $10,000 a month by the time I graduated from college.

The race was on!

The $100 in My Bank Account

I sat and pondered what I was going to do. I had exactly $100 to my name. My options were very limited. With such limited funds, it wasn't like I could just go out and buy a McDonald's franchise!

So, what now?

My journey began and ended very quickly – all in one night.

That was the first night I felt the real pinch of being an entrepreneur. I was all alone and had no idea what I was doing. I had no one to guide me, no one to save me from my mistakes.

I had only one friend left who could help me.

A Life-Changing Google Search

I decided to turn to my best friend, Google.com. I ran straight to Google and typed in these cliché words:

What happened after that was very frustrating. I was chauffeured into scam after scam. I read about exciting opportunities to make money by stuffing envelopes. I learned of many "life-changing" MLM companies that seemed to disappear in weeks. I even was shocked to learn that I could simply make money by "filling out surveys."

Fortunately, I took some time to research these opportunities and find that they were not real. After all, I only had $100 to invest. My life depended on this $100.

I was becoming very frustrated, but something inside me told me to keep searching. Something told me that the answer was just around the corner and if I quit now, all my efforts would be wasted.

As I kept my search on, I finally landed on a discussion board that was dedicated to online entrepreneurs.

Online entrepreneur. Now, what in the world is that?

I started reading post after post and became absolutely enthralled with what I was seeing. Day after day, I was meeting people through this discussion board who were claiming (and proving) to make anywhere from $300 a day to even $10,000 a day! They were all doing this sitting at home using just one computer. They had no employees, no offices, and no headaches.

They seemed honest, genuine, and very helpful. I was sold.

These entrepreneurs were cashing in big time by just publishing information on the Internet and selling it using some simple models. There wasn't just one person doing it; there were hundreds!

That was the day I decided on my new career. I was going to be an online entrepreneur.

Eighteen Months Wasted and $100 Lost

Unfortunately, back when I started in 2002 there was no program like The Profit Academy to follow step by step. There was no Circle of Profit that could be copied and pasted. Back then, everyone found their own system by hook and crook. In the process, some succeeded and many failed.

Having full confidence in my own abilities, I ventured to start my new career very fast. I figured "Hey, I'm smart; if they can do it, so can I." From what I had seen, the formula was very simple.

1. Find a topic you're good at or passionate about.
2. Create a digital product with information on that topic.

3. Put it up online and wait for your millions.

I never stopped to consider the missing pieces. I never stopped to consider that almost all successful businesses were built from models and systems that could be copied. After months of learning, I took a topic I was good at and I just took blind action.

I spent seven months painfully learning how to do each step myself. I spent seven months applying techniques the best I knew how. I also spent the little $100 I had. I was absolutely sure that I was about to break into millions.

I was convinced that I had figured out a "niche" or topic to create a product on that no one else had ever thought about. Having no system, no training, and no coach, I tried to just do it.

Seven months invested and the day had come. The day had come that I would launch my digital product and laugh my way to the bank. However, something was missing. The day I launched my digital product, something crucial was missing.

I wasn't getting a single sale.

I hadn't made a dime and over 24 hours had passed. Two days passed, a week passed, a month passed. I had made absolutely nothing.

Not only had I lost my $100 but I had even spent $500 on a credit card. For the first time in my life, I was in debt!

I was heartbroken. My dream for instant millions had come crashing down. However, as I've already told you, I wasn't one to give up so easily. I was determined to find my mistake and try a different model. One way or the other, I was going to succeed as an online entrepreneur!

I had all the determination in the world, but that never changed the one thing that I did not have: *a system*.

No matter how many months passed and no matter how hard I worked, I continued to fail because I never had a model to actually follow. I had no one holding my hand.

Quickly, the seven months became 18 months and I had yet to make even a dime in profit. I had easily worked for more than 3,000 hours and had nothing to show for it other than losses.

The Final Night

I was ready to quit. I was embarrassed, disheartened, and exhausted.

I was beginning to get convinced that building an online business around digital products was a dream too good to be true. Had I been lied to yet again? Was business not for me? Should I have stayed my course to become a doctor? What would I ever tell my parents? What about all my friends who were desperately waiting say, "I told you so"?

After months of searching, there was only one thing that was left for me to try. That night, I decided to make this my absolute final attempt to becoming an online entrepreneur.

"If this doesn't work either, then I'm done. I'll go get some J.O.B. and do it the way that everyone else tells me to do it. I'll accept my defeat and never try anything like this again."

That night I worked until 5:00 a.m. I messaged every Internet entrepreneur I had ever spoken to. I read as much as I could. I put together as many pieces of the puzzle as I could find and I spent countless hours testing a strategy that was built around one of my true passions.

I remember typing away at my keyboard, barely staying awake. I worked until my last breath and finally retreated to sleep. This was the final hour. That night, I remember praying myself right into sleep. I knew that the next morning would be a key deciding moment in my life.

That night I created a model that was the simplest of them all. It was just one step.

Six hours later, my eyes opened. I sprang out of bed and nearly fell flat as I plunged towards my computer, still half asleep. I had to know right away. Had it worked?

With chills running down my back, I remember logging into my account to see that I had made $300 in profit while I slept. I rubbed my eyes and drew my face closer to the screen just to confirm that I was not hallucinating.

Nope.

Sure enough, for the first time in my life, I had made a profit: my first $300 as an online entrepreneur.

Olga's Story: Making That First Buck

Olga came to me as a student in one of my classes. As a bonus twist, she was an exchange student who had come to the States from Germany.

She wasn't someone who was down on her luck or in a desperate situation. She was married to a great guy and was already pretty happy. She just wanted more in life and wanted to reach a fuller potential. She simply wanted to live the life of her dreams.

As she first started, she actually got stuck at one point and even struggled a little bit for a moment. Her husband was a little skeptical of the whole Internet marketing business model, but being the loving, caring guy he is, he stood by his wife and fully supported her.

Olga was so excited to be doing this. She was one of those people with a twinkle in her eye; she tried and tried and followed the system and in a short period of time she was right on track and doing well. All it took for her was being introduced to the Profit Academy system.

After months of struggling, it was this very system that led to her major break-through.

She still talks about the chills she had down her spine when she generated her first $1 in profit. She couldn't believe her eyes. Till this day she says she will never forget that feeling. That was the day that she knew her wildest dreams were officially possible.

She knew without a shadow of doubt that the Profit Academy system would be able to help her turn her true passion into $1 Million or even much more.

Today, she's growing every single month. She works on her business part-time and sees her income rising day by day. She says she couldn't see herself doing anything different. Ever.

Olga has been so successful and we were so impressed that we invited her to be part of our team. *The student has now become the teacher.*

The Birth of The Circle of Profit

Little did I know back then, but the Circle of Profit had just been born. Step #1 of Phase #1 was fully in action. In the last 18 months, I had tried countless strategies to generate a profit online. I had worked for over 3,000 hours.

It was shocking and even slightly infuriating to learn that out of everything I had tried, it was actually the simplest and easiest model of them all that finally led me to profit.

The crazy part?

It only took me a few hours that night to start the entire process and even make my first profit. I was now a believer. I had confirmed that the dream of building an online business around my passions was not only doable, but pretty darn simple.

The time had come that I poured my heart and soul into this new strategy. I wanted to see how far I could push it. I wanted to see just how much I could actually make from it.

Would I finally make good on my promise to my friends? Would I make my first $10,000 before I even graduated from College?

From Thousands To Millions

I could quickly see the potential in what I had found. My first and foremost goal remained to reach $10,000 a month but I was already dreaming of the millions I knew could be earned! I had anticipated the $10,000 mark taking me at least 6 months to reach. However, much to my surprise, I found myself reaching my life-long dream within the first 60 days!

During those 60 days I solely focused on building and gaining subscribers to an Email Newsletter I had started. By simply putting up a one page website (built within a few clicks), I began to use simple and automated techniques to attract subscribers to my website. I was basically attracting people to my website who shared in my passion! I would then offer to give them free training and promise to send them quality content on a regular basis in exchange for their Email address.

With a simple promise such as that, I began to collect thousands of Email addresses from individuals who were eager to open the Emails I sent them. The model I followed was as simple as it gets:

I began to build a relationship with my new subscribers by following a simple pattern of emails. It's important to note that I was never a good writer; writing was the only subject I nearly failed in school.

I worked through my writing challenges, testing many strategies until I nailed it down to an easy formula. The first step of the Circle of Profit was officially born, but I quickly knew that it was time to grow and time to scale.

Within six months from the day I made my first $300, my income had gone from $10,000 a month to more than $30,000 a month. At this point, I still had a very simple system that was managed fully in less than 60 minutes a day. At this point, I was still a full-time student and running my business during my breaks between classes.

If I could generate $10,000 a month with such little effort, surely I could easily scale it into a $1 million or more business!

As I perfected the Phase 1 of the Circle of Profit (explained in detail later in this book) I stumbled onto what soon became Phase 2: releasing my own digital product. I would just take information and package it together in one place. I quickly found that hundreds, if not thousands, of people were willing to pay for this information.

My products soon became a raging success. Almost overnight, my income jumped from $30,000 a month to $60,000 a month simply because I had created my own product. Before I knew it, I was fast marching towards my $1 million dream!

Fast-forward a few years:

My Boring and Repetitive Formula to $10 Million

I continued to rinse and repeat the same Circle and my profits continued to grow. I generated $1 million my very first year in business. After that, it was simply a matter of applying the simple formula, day in and day out. The more times I applied the Circle of Profit, the more my profits grew.

I was living my dream. I graduated from college and immediately began traveling the world. I was speaking on some of the biggest stages around the world sharing my story. I was being featured in *BusinessWeek* magazine and *Inc 500* was knocking down my door.

Six years flew by and I was sitting at the gates of generating $10 million in just one year. I had grown to this level from $0, all the while using the Circle of Profit. My business was booming so fast that I actually grew bored with it. The Circle of Profit had become so repetitive and easy that I actually began to seek more complicated solutions, just for the sake of seeking them. My search was unfounded and would prove to be a mistake that nearly cost me my life.

The Price for Not Following the Circle of Profit: Bankruptcy

It had taken me six years to build my business from nothing to $10 million a year. However, generating income had become so simple and repetitive that I actually sought other routes. I felt if making $10 Million was so easy, surely with a more complicated model, I could generate $100 million!

I began to hire an expensive team.

I built offices around the world.

I poured money into becoming a star so I could live the jet-set lifestyle of a *Fortune 500* CEO. I began to feel I was absolutely untouchable.

The bottom line is that I completely and foolishly turned my back to the beautiful Circle of Profit that had helped me achieve my dreams. I was searching for something more complicated simply because I felt the Circle was too simple and easy.

In 2008 when the economy crashed, so did I. I had turned a blind eye to the only system that had ever made me millions. Unfortunately, I was not alone. Many great online entrepreneurs found themselves on the same ill-sought journey that I was on, also paying the same high price.

I went from making $10 million a year in sales to $1.7 million in debt. I owed everyone money: banks, credit cards, vendors, my family, my friends, and many more.

I found my phone besieged by debt collectors. I couldn't keep up with the expenses but I refused to change my model. I was still convinced that the answer was in a more complicated system. Today I think back and always ask myself, "Had I only turned back to the simple Circle of Profit…"

My life began to fall apart. I was hospitalized. I was hiding. I was nearly ready to give up on everything. That was until one day in

Amsterdam, when I was carried off a plane on a stretcher.

Nearly Dying on an Airplane

I was at the Amsterdam airport, scheduled to fly back home. However, the 24 hours before this flight, I had become very ill. I'd had severe health problems for well over a decade at this point, but my health had never been worse than during these troubled times of debt. I was constantly under debilitating stress and my condition was worsening.

It all peaked in Amsterdam.

The entire night before my flight, I found myself sweating in bed and rapidly losing energy. I later discovered that I had been bleeding internally the entire time. I had lost nearly 50% of the blood in my body!

That day, as I walked towards my flight, I could feel myself getting sicker and sicker. Within minutes of boarding the flight, my state of consciousness began to falter. I don't remember most of what happened after that, except this:

I woke up and I was being strapped onto a stretcher. I was being carried downstairs and as I could see, I was departing the plane. Apparently, the plane had pulled back from the gate just as I had completely lost consciousness. I never got to thank my mysterious savior, the passenger sitting next to me.

This passenger had the intuition to discern that I was not simply sleeping, but that I had lost consciousness. He apparently waved down the flight attendant and the plane was stopped.

The next thing I remember is finding myself strapped down to a bed with multiple devices connected to me. There were so many devices on me that I could not even move. I was alone in a foreign country and on what seemed to be my deathbed. That day, I remember thinking to myself:

> *"The whole reason I got into business was financial **freedom**. Now, I find myself literally strapped to this bed and barely able to move. This is the farthest from freedom anyone can get. It's time for a change; I can't go out like this!"*

I recovered enough to fly back home and immediately went into action. I began to close offices and I released nearly every employee I had hired. The moment had come. I had to discover just what had gone wrong. Why was I suddenly bankrupt and dying when just two years ago I had been swimming in millions and living the life of my dreams?

The answer: I had turned my back to the Circle of Profit.

As I sat in my dark office the night before I had to turn over the keys, I made a commitment to myself: I would go back to the Circle of Profit, the simple system that had helped me build my first $10 million. This time, I would not turn my back to it. I was going to use this proven system to get myself back on my feet.

Back to $10 Million in 16 Months

What happened after that was surreal. I dug my heels in, simplified my business (and my life) and went back to the simple basics of the Circle of Profit. I forced myself to start all over again. I went back to Phase 1 and decided to give it everything I had.

When I restarted, I was $1.7 million in debt. I was able to completely pay off that debt in just 12 months. Furthermore, I found myself sitting again on a $10 million a year business within just 16 months of the day I had decided to go back to the Circle of Profit.

What had once taken me six years to do, I had now done in 16 months.

That was also the day I decided it was time for me to teach this to the world. That brings us to today and to this book.

The Moral of This Story

The Circle of Profit is simple and redundant. Use it.

Don't try to reinvent something that works well. Just copy and paste the steps you are taught and focus on execution. The simplicity of this Circle is a gift. It is this very gift that allows you to focus on your life while letting the business run itself.

You can use the following system to make $100,000 a year or even $10 million a year. The system is completely flexible to your life and your needs.

From this moment on, your success, your future is completely up to you and only you. If you just promise to work hard and let my team of trainers (inside the Profit Academy) show you the way, your new life is waiting for you just around the corner.

How I Finally Quit My Boring Job
Student: Willie Laney

I thought I had finally made it.

I had enrolled in countless courses and done everything I could. I even invested a lot of time and created my first product. I did everything I knew how to. However, I still spent every day completely confused.

I just wasn't seeing the success as fast as I thought I would. What was worse is that I had wasted more than $5,000 getting my business online, all the wrong way!

I only made a couple hundred bucks!

After all the hard work, countless hours of my life and over $5,000 invested, I was no where. My dream life felt like it was even farther way! I finally started to have doubts. I was convinced that maybe being an online Entrepreneur wasn't really for me?

That was when I stumbled across Anik Singal. Anik seemed to be creating a long line of success stories behind him. He himself was generating over $10 Million a year using a system that seemed very simple! I didn't know what, but something felt different about him. I was excited…

He was the EXACT opposite.

Unlike any of the other courses I had experienced, I could immediately tell that Anik really cared. He really wanted to help people like me! I decided to take my life into my own hands and I took action. I became a student of his and immediately began studying his Profit Academy system.

It was super simple!

It was almost like copying and pasting what he did. I finally found myself understanding every detail about my business. The best part was that in less than 10 days of following his system, I generated over $1,200!

I had spent months and months to make only $200 and here I was able to use his system to generate over $1,200 in just 10 days! I was hooked.

I worked harder than ever. I learned more. I completed all his training. I always took action. Before I knew it, I found myself resigning at my job; a job where I earned over $80,000 a year!

A FREE Invitation That Will Change Your Life

As I've said before, I am very committed to your success. I really want you to have everything you need to succeed in your online business. To help you further, I have invested a lot of money to bring you some amazing free training that's worth at least $1,497.

It's called the **Profit Workshop**.

I'm hosting three LIVE training sessions. I have actually built an entire LIVE studio for this. I will be using every presentation tool at my disposal to dissect the entire Profit Academy system down for you!

I will also be joined by some of our most successful students who have used every piece of the Profit Academy training to become runaway successes. They will be available to answer your questions and give you everything you need.

GOAL: *How To Turn Your Passions Into $1 Million*

February 23rd – 8:00 p.m. Eastern
Profit Workshop #1 – How to Quickly Generate $100,000 With a Tiny System

February 26th – 8:00 p.m. Eastern
Profit Workshop #2 – How to Turn That $100,000 Into $500,000 in an Instant

March 3rd – 8:00 p.m. Eastern
Profit Workshop #3 – The Final Secret to $1 Million

Among these three free LIVE training sessions, you're going to become a master at building your own online digital business. I've compressed more than 13 years of education into these three workshops.

No matter what you do, don't miss these sessions. Even if you miss the LIVE presentations, go to www.FreeProfitWorkshop.com and absorb the replays. Trust me: This training is life changing.

You will also have a very limited opportunity to join our Profit Academy program. It is highly limited and not for everyone. After you learn from our LIVE workshop trainings, you will get a chance to see if you are actually ready for this fast-paced, hands-on training with my team and me.

www.FreeProfitWorkshop.com

Register for your free seat right away!

Chapter 2
The Digital Gold Rush

"Small opportunities are often the beginning of great enterprises." - Demosthenes

In this chapter, I'm going to formally introduce you to the powerful Circle of Profit, a system you can copy and paste to turn your passion into $1 million.

The Circle of Profit is very simple at its core:

1. Find other people like yourself.
2. Provide them with valuable information.
   a. You can promote information others are selling.
   b. You can promote your own information.
3. Profit ("Rinse and Repeat").

I want to emphasize that the entire Circle is fueled by one word: *Value*. The more value you provide, the faster and bigger your business will grow. Through this book and my Free Profit Workshop (www.FreeProfitWorkshop.com) you are going to have the entire template placed right into your lap.

My team and I have worked for years to get this entire system down into simple steps that anyone can copy. Even if you have no experience, no technical background, or have never considered owning a business, you can do this. I am about to amaze you.

If you are serious about building a life full of dreams and financial freedom, get ready to take action. It's time for you to pick up the shovel and start digging!

The Modern-Day California Gold Rush

There has never been a better time to create this kind of digital business. More and more people are turning to the Internet for information. The best part is that these people are not just looking for free information; there are millions around the world happy to pay for it!

I'm calling it the modern-day California Gold Rush.

I'm serious.

Many people make the mistake of thinking that Internet opportunities have come and gone, but they are very wrong. The opportunity to create millions on the Internet with nothing but your computer is alive and well. It is better than ever before.

Today is an even better day to launch your own online business than it was 10 years ago. If I'd had the kind of access you do today, I would have achieved my results 1,000% faster. That is precisely why I have created the Profit Academy. I want to make sure you never struggle the way I did.

Nick's Story: The Power of Taking Action

This story is one of my all time favorites. Nick was a young guy, still a little wet behind the ears, and he had his whole life and the world ahead of him. He didn't have a clue about Internet marketing and was a total "newbie."

Nick was actually a military pilot for the UK and was already set in his career. But like so many of us, he wanted more from life.

What stood out to me most about Nick was the joy in his voice when he talked about how easy the system was.
He would say over and over, *"All you have to do is take action. Do the steps and it will work for you. Just copy, paste, and repeat. The trick is in the doing."*

And you know what? Nick is absolutely right. The trick is in the doing! If you do the steps, you almost can't help but succeed.

That's the power of Profit Academy. It's a drop-dead simple system and to make it work, all you have to do is *take action and do it. If you follow the steps the system will work.*

Consider this.

Twenty years ago if you wanted to learn something, you'd go to the library or bookstore and pick up a book. If there was new information on a topic, it had to go through a long publication process (an average of 18 months). By the time that new information came out, it was mostly outdated!

Today is very different.

We live in the Information Age. The greatest industry in the world today is **information**. Those with access to information and the ability to distribute it the fastest are the ones who are poised to be our next millionaires and billionaires.

The day of physical books is quickly disappearing. The speed at which everyone is seeking Information using only the Internet is growing faster than ever.

In 2012, Amazon CEO Jeff Bezos announced that Amazon's sales of digital books had surpassed their sales of physical books.

Just look at how fast the Internet is growing around the world. In the last 10 years, the number of people using the Internet has grown by 600%. It's estimated that there are more than three billion people now with access to the Internet.

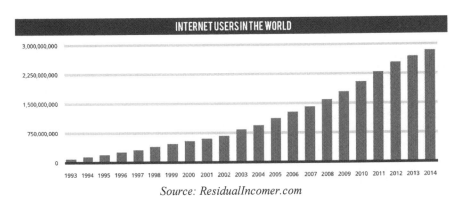
Source: ResidualIncomer.com

Even better, studies have shown that over 62% of everyone on the Internet primarily uses it to gain information.

* * *

USES OF THE INTERNET IN

Percentage of users

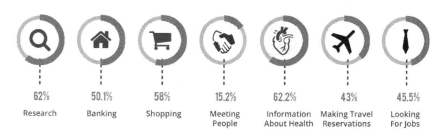

62%	50.1%	58%	15.2%	62.2%	43%	45.5%
Research	Banking	Shopping	Meeting People	Information About Health	Making Travel Reservations	Looking For Jobs

These numbers are only growing. It's estimated that by 2020, there will be **five billion** people online. In the United States alone, the market for just eBooks alone (one form of digital information) was worth $270 million in 2008. By 2014, that figure had already grown to $5.69 billion. If you do the math, that averages to over 250% growth per year!

What's even better is that this number could grow to $8.69 billion by 2018.

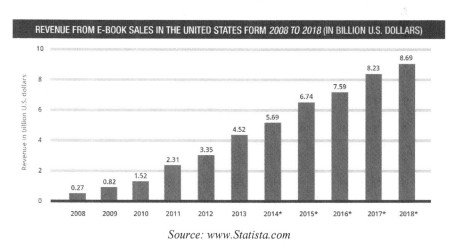

Source: www.Statista.com

Imagine having just a tiny sliver of that amount of money. This is why I'm telling you it's a perfect time to start your digital online business.

Just think:

This book is a perfect example of the importance and power of information. You have chosen to read this book because you know that the system in it can quickly change your life. Although you and I might never meet face to face, the Internet is allowing me to teach you everything I know.

Many of my students are now earning millions without ever having met me.

"I feel like you've virtually been with me through every step. It's amazing how you've addressed every question, skepticism and doubts I've ever had. I've read many books and listened to countless audio books but I always felt lost.

Not anymore!

Thank you, Anik!" ~ Pamela Najera

This book is information through the written word.

What Do You Need To Start

It's very simple.

The only physical tools you need are the following:
- Access to a computer.
- An Internet connection.
- One hour a day.

I think it is fair to assume that you already have all three of these tool. If you are reading this book, it's unlikely that you got your hands on it without having both a computer and Internet access. And I firmly believe that we all have at least one hour a day to make our dreams come true.

Beyond that, you just need resilient drive. Get ready to soak in every piece of training that I am making available to you. Take action on the training. Most of all, if you are really ready to attach some rocket boosters to the process, join The Profit Academy and let my team hold your hands through the entire process.

How I Ran My Business From The I.C.U.

Back in 2005, I was in the middle of scaling and building my business when an unlikely event happened. Unexpectedly, my physical body started breaking down on me.

My physical health reached the point that I was admitted to the hospital and placed in the ICU. There I was, one moment fighting to grow my business and the next, fighting to save my life. And I definitely couldn't give up on either of them.

So, now I was faced with a whole new challenge: How do you run a business from a hospital bed? I was in no condition to just get up and go use a computer. Even if I could, it was not allowed. They do not allow any electronics inside the I.C.U.

Lucky for me I didn't have a typical day job. If I had, there is no way my business would have survived. My career would have ended. I would have had zero income. I cringe at even the thought of what would have happened to me when I came out of the hospital.

However, thanks to my online business and my simple system, I have the luxury of being able to run my business from anywhere in the World! I can run my business from home, from Starbucks, the beach and in this case, even the I.C.U.

Now this next part is a bit funny. I'm smiling as I write this, just thinking about it.

* * *

Like I said, there were no computers or laptops allowed in the ICU.
So, here's what I did. I had my friend sneak in my BlackBerry phone
right into the I.C.U. and leave it underneath my pillow. It was a small
device and very discrete. This phone would be my only available tool
to run my business. The question was, how would I do it?

Late at night, once the lights were off, I would hide under the covers
and secretly
use my blackberry to text and email people. So, in about an hour a
day, I was running and managing my entire business "undercover,"
literally.

While in the I.C.U. for over three months, I was able to run my entire
business using my blackberry cell phone. I generated over $450,000
in sales, all while I could barely stand-up without my heart rate
spiking.

Can you imagine any business model that is simpler and easier to
build. If this model can be run from a hospital bed, imagine what you
can do with it!

Chapter 3

What Is A Digital Business

"Systems will either empower you to succeed or set you up to fail. Make the decision to build your daily success systems." - John Di Lemme

Here it is. The Circle of Profit. The only system you ever need to build a ragingly successful online business!

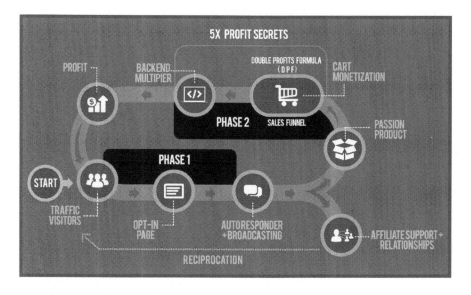

The Quickest Explanation

As you can see, there are many pieces to the Circle of Profit. The rest of this book is all about dissecting each of the pieces. Before we get to the details, no matter what piece we are talking about, always remember this simple diagram:

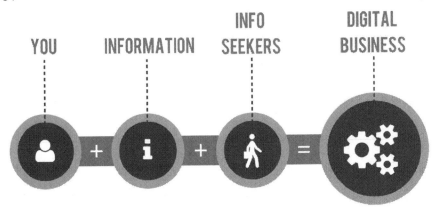

There are three parts to a digital business.
- The first part of a digital business is **you**.
- The second part of a digital business is **the information you have**.
- The third part of a digital business is **the other person who is seeking information**. I like to call them *info seekers*.

The Circle of Profit connects you and your information with these info seekers. The connection of all three parts is where profit is created. In the end, this is all that a digital business is.

Weight-Loss Example

People often ask me, "What is teaching your passion?" or "How do you teach your passion?" So here's an example to make it easier for you to understand.

Let's say you were heavy and you decided that you were going to lose some weight. You read up on diet and exercise and you found everything that you could by going through thousands of pages of information. After learning, you decided to take your new knowledge and put it into action!

* * *

Suddenly, you started to lose weight.

Not only did you lose weight, but also you began to love learning more about health and fitness. Before you knew it, your friends were calling you. Your family was calling you. You found yourself consistently giving others advice on how to lose weight.

All the while, you had lost over twenty pounds using your newfound secrets!

You didn't even know but you had suddenly found a new passion!

All of a sudden you fell in love with the idea of immersing yourself, day and night, in the world of health and fitness. You were already teaching it to all your friends. That is when you read this book and it finally clicked.

Why not follow the Circle of Profit and start teaching the World. Not only would you love every waking moment of your every day, but you would start to making millions of dollars doing it!

That's how your passion can be turned into profits.

The Three Things Any Online Passion Business Needs

The Circle of Profit uses three very simple tools to create a profitable online business around your passion. These are simple, straightforward tools and every one of my Profit Academy students master all three in a matter of just a few weeks.

Tool #1:

You need something called an ***email list***. An *email list* is just a group of people who have come to your one-page website (*which you build using click-click technology*) and decide to give you their email addresses. I will show you a way to easily bribe hundreds of thousands of people to give you their email addresses. Imagine having your own magazine, except it's 1,000 times easier to get subscribers and even easier than that to send them content. You also barely have any costs.

We'll get into more detail on this very soon.

Tool #2:

The next tool we use is an ***information product***. This is what I mean when I say a "digital product." Although you can also have software products, our focus will be on information products. Information products are books or courses on particular topics.

The book you are reading right now is an example of an information product. It's a book that is helping you start your own business and create financial freedom in your life. There are many kinds of information products; you can get a good example if you also register for my Free Profit Workshop at www.FreeProfitWorkshop.com

Tool #3:

Finally, the Circle of Profit relies on ***affiliate marketing***. Affiliate marketing is when you promote other people's products— usually digital information products—and make a percentage of each sale. You can build a very profitable business without ever creating your own product! Many existing information products are excellent and pay upwards of 75% commission. You actually can earn more than even the product owner by just following a few simple steps we reveal.

How a New Business Was Automatically Born

Here's an example of how I personally cashed in on one of my passions. For as long as I can remember, I've always been interested in and fascinated with the workings of the mind. I was always reading, always learning, and dissecting every thing I could get my hands on related to the subject.

I couldn't get enough of it. The more I read, the more I learned, and the more I wanted to learn. It got to the point that I had learned so much that I would tell anybody about it who would listen to me. That's how much I enjoyed it.

One day I got the idea to start a newsletter. I figured this would be a place to get all my ideas out and I could share my point of views on the various books I've read and products I've used—just a place to share my joy with others.

First there were a few subscribers. Then a few hundred, and then a few thousand. Before I knew it, things really began to take off.

I knew I was onto something and that's when it hit me: Why not sell or endorse the products that I was already using and enjoying. They helped and worked for me and I knew it would for others as well!

Just like that, a new business was born.

Now, if you look at the Circle of Profit diagram again, you will see that every part of this diagram can be grouped into any of these three tools.

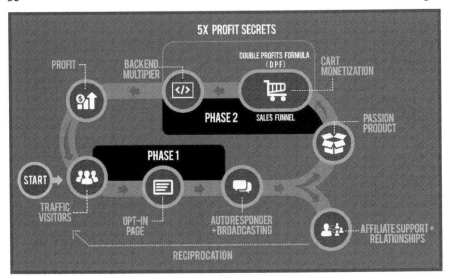

The Two Phases of Your Online Empire

As you can see in the diagram, there are two phases to the Circle of Profit. Phase 1 is all about building up your email list and Phase 2 is about creating and promoting your own information products.

Remember, even if you stop at Phase 1, you can make great profits. However, if you want to turn your passion into $1 million, you will need to master Phase 2 as well.

The only catch is that in order to properly build Phase 2, you are required to go through Phase 1 first. No matter what kind of online empire you want to build, Phase 1 is the most important first step.

Phase 1 starts with one main task: You need to discover your profitable passion. This phase is pretty much a copy and paste system; however, you have to first make sure you are addressing a profitable topic and that your particular passion has a business model behind it.

Chapter 4
Finding Your Profitable Passion

"Follow you passion, be prepared to work hard and sacrifice, and above all, don't let anyone limit your dreams." - Donovan Bailey

There is nothing more liberating than doing what you love. It breaks my heart when I meet people every day who absolutely despise their careers. Even worse than that is when I meet people who are considered incredibly successful but who are completely miserable. They are trapped in their career because of the money, but are riddled with stress and unhappiness because they lack passion.

Surrounding ourselves with our passions is the number-one way to live a truly free and fulfilling life. Life is much more fulfilling when you are waking up every day excited to work. Even if you have millions of dollars in your bank account, until you are surrounded by a life of your passion, you will never truly be free.

Trust me; I've been on both sides. Today, I'm blessed because I get to wake up every day and do what I love: I get to spend every moment of my day talking about and teaching entrepreneurship. I get to go to sleep every night knowing that I helped thousands of people chase their dreams. There is absolutely no better way to live my life!

Passion: The Key To Your Success

Of course, to create a passion business, you need to know what you are passionate about. The good news is that you can build your business around just about any passion.

Personally, my passion is entrepreneurship. I love giving people the tools to make their dreams a reality. To this day, there is nothing that brings a bigger smile to my face than when I get an email from a student. The emails tell me about how different their life is now and how they are living a life of their dreams, all because they applied the teachings of the Profit Academy program.

When I first started my business, my focus had always been immersing and surrounding myself with entrepreneurship. Little did I know, it was most likely that very fact that led to my amazing growth. I was able to take $100 and turn it into millions even when I had no experience or prior knowledge. I loved what I was doing and I was truly passionate about every moment of my life.

However, the day came when I began to turn my back on my passions.

As I mentioned earlier, I felt the Circle of Profit was too simple and I began to chase more complicated models. I wanted to grow even faster. I wanted to live the lifestyle of a *Fortune 500* CEO. In order to do this, I began to hire a big team. I opened multiple offices. Before I knew it, I'd left my passions behind. Now, I was never working with entrepreneurs; rather, I was focusing on trying to manage my employees and cover my expenses.

Before I knew it, I hated my life. I hated my business. It all became a burden.

I started trying to build digital businesses in various niches for which I had zero passion. It came as a surprise to me then that no matter how much money I threw at those businesses, they kept failing. Well, fast-forward to today and I completely understand why that happened.

Passion is your key to success. Remember that and you will have won 90% of the battle towards success.

Even though I had fallen into $1.7 million of debt, nearly bankrupt and lying on my deathbed, passion brought me back to life. When I decided to go back to the simple Circle of Profit, I fully recovered and was back on top of the world in just 16 months.

However, is it enough to just have passion?

What if your passion is going to the lake and skipping rocks? Is it really viable to build a business on that topic? Unfortunately, the answer is no.

Once you have a list of what inspires passion from you, we now have to put it up against the "business test." We have to make sure that we choose the passion that has the most commercial value so that we can profit the most.

Choosing the right topic to launch a business was one of the first lessons I ever learned (the hard way) about 13 years ago.

How I Wasted Seven Months of My Life

When I first started trying to learn how to make money online, I was in a rush. Thirteen years ago, we didn't have structured training courses such as The Profit Academy, I had to do it on my own. Well, I rushed it. I made a deadly assumption and it cost me seven months of my life!

I basically figured out that people were taking a topic that they're good at. They were then writing a product on it. They were putting it up on the Internet and suddenly, money was pouring in!

I figured, *"hey I'm really good at studying and finding tricks to ace exams without studying hard at all!"* Plus, there are millions of college students, I must be onto something.

I was even more excited to see that there was no competition in the market! I thought I had just struck gold. I was convinced I would be a millionaire before college was even over!

But…

…the product was a flop.

I spent seven months of my life barking up the wrong tree the entire time. I had never taken the time to truly understand the difference between a "passion" and a "profitable passion."

Luckily, you don't have to make the same mistake!

Is Your Passion Profitable?

So what kind of passion is profitable and capable of turning into $1 million? There are really only three requirements that are key. These factors should never be ignored or else you will set yourself up for failure.

1. Passion.

I know, I know; we keep saying this. I'm not trying to irritate you; I'm just trying to really drive it home. Here's why: For the first few months in business, times will always be hard. You will hit obstacles, your profit will be lower, and you will need dedication to get through it.

If, when the times get tough, you are building a business around your passion, you will stand a stronger chance of surviving, if for no other reason than because you are enjoying the process. Most people who fail do so because they start their business only for the money. If they don't see profits in the first few days, they lose all their motivation.

Don't be one of these people!

2. Audience.

You want to make sure there are a lot of people in the world who share your passion. For example, if you have a passion for a very rare type of food found in a remote part of the world, that's great. However, not enough people in the world even know about this food to share your passion.

You will be fighting an uphill battle right from the start. We don't want to start there. I always say, make sure there are at least a million people in the world who share your passion.

If you want to learn the step-by-step process to using some simple tools that can quickly tell you the size of your market – make sure you register for the Free Profit Workshop. I'm going to show you how to do all this LIVE!

www.FreeProfitWorkshop.com

3. **Money.**

Having an audience is one thing. You have to assure that your audience is capable of spending money on your topic. This was the greatest mistake I made when I first started 13 years ago. I found "how to study in college" and obviously, it's a massive market. However, college students would never want to spend $47 on a product like that. They would rather take their small allowance and splurge it on beer and pizza.

I learned this particular lesson the hard way.

The information has to be valuable enough to your target audience that they will be willing enough to pull out their credit cards for it.

There is ONE final test that can make your life much easier. You don't even have to think about the first three metrics as long as this fourth one exists.

4. **Competition.**

When I first found the "how to study in college" niche, I found absolutely no competition. There was no one on the Internet selling this kind of information. There were tons of free articles, but no one selling a course.

I assumed I was brilliant.

Out of the millions of online entrepreneurs, I was the only one who had thought of this idea! I was convinced I was going to be a millionaire before I even graduated from college.

I spent seven months preparing this product and when I finally released it 30 days into my marketing, I had not even made one sale.

It was that day that I created a simple rule: Competition is good. I never recommend going into a market that has no competition. If others are selling information similar to yours, that is excellent for you. Here's why:

- They have validated the market. You know there is profit to be made.

- You can market THEIR products as an affiliate.
- They can become your top partners later and they can promote your product for you, too.

There you have it. Assuring that your passion is capable of turning into $1 million is simple and easy. Follow these rules and you will be golden.

Passions That Are Very Profitable

Just to help you get started and to give you some ideas, here's a starting point. The best topics to launch an online business in tend to be in the big three:

1. **Health** (Physical, Spiritual, and Emotional)
2. **Wealth** (Business, Investing, etc.)
3. **Relationships** (Marriage, Dating, Parenting, etc.)

This does not mean that these are the only three. There are plenty of niches outside these; however, in my career I have seen a bulk of great success come from these three areas. Here are some more detailed examples to get you thinking:

- **Weight loss**
- **Bodybuilding**
- **Healthy eating**
- **Dating advice**
- **Investing**
- **Real estate**
- **Electronics / gadgets**
- **Gaming**
- **Pets**
- **Finding a job**
- **Panic attacks**
- **Reiki**
- **Hypnosis**
- **Divorce**
- **Superfoods**

As long as you have passion, a big audience with money, and existing competition in the market, you can turn any viable topic into $1 million using the Circle of Profit.

Chapter 5
Time To Start Building

All right, it's time to get started and get your business off the ground! I hope you're excited. That future of financial freedom and the ability to shape your dream life is right at your fingertips. All you need to do is follow the simple steps I'm laying out. Don't take any shortcuts and don't try to re-invent the wheel.

As I mentioned before, the digital information market is a $10 billion industry (by 2020). If you can carve out even a small slice of that, you can live a life that most people can only fantasize about. The key to carving out your little slice is the Circle of Profit!

Starting in our next section, we're going to dive into the Circle and go through each piece in detail. You're about to get 13 years of knowledge within just a few chapters, so please be sure to pay close attention.

Many times we also hear from students who want more hands-on help. I want to assure you that we are here (my entire team and me) to do anything for you that we possibly can. If you want more training and more handholding you have two more resources you can access. I suggest you do both of them; our most successful and serious students have:

#1 – Free Profit Workshop (Value, $1,497)

- February 23, 2015 – 8:00 p.m. Eastern
- February 26 2015 – 8:00 p.m. Eastern
- March 2, 2015 – 8:00 p.m. Eastern

Mark these dates down and make sure you are present for the LIVE training. I have been preparing this training for over one year now. You're going to be blown away. Through the three training sessions, I will show you just how to go from where you are now to turning your passion into $1 million.

* * *

www.FreeProfitWorkshop.com

#2 – Join Us Inside the Profit Academy

We will open our doors for our next class on February 23. However, we are highly limited and you have to qualify to gain admission. Our most successful students are graduates of this program. As a matter of fact, all of my top trainers are graduates of this very program.

If you are 100% serious and ready to put full focus on your online business, then on February 23, I highly recommend you join us and let us guide you by the hand.

You have no excuses now. I'm taking personal responsibility for your success. All I ask is that you simply take action, step by step, on what we are teaching.

All right, let's keep going. It's time to dissect The Circle of Profit.

Section 2

Your Information Empire

Chapter 6
Crash Course To The Circle Of Profit

"If you can dream it, you can do it." – Walt Disney

In this chapter, I'm going to give you the bird's-eye view of the Circle of Profit. As you know, it is a simple, proven approach to making money on line by doing what you're passionate about. It's the same model that built me multiple million-dollar businesses.

And not just me.

It's the same model that has helped thousands of my students from every background imaginable achieve complete financial freedom. Believe me when I say this: If we can do it, you can do it.

"This course has been life changing. I find myself in awe of how simple, but powerful all of the advice is! After getting through the last lesson I completed, I really sat back and thought about the other programs I have tried. They didn't even come close!

~ Lisa Parker

In Chapter 4, we reviewed what makes for a *profitable* passion. By now, you should be starting to get an idea of which passion you want to pursue.

Write down those profitable passion ideas. Keep these ideas in front of you and let's dive into the Circle of Profit, piece by piece.

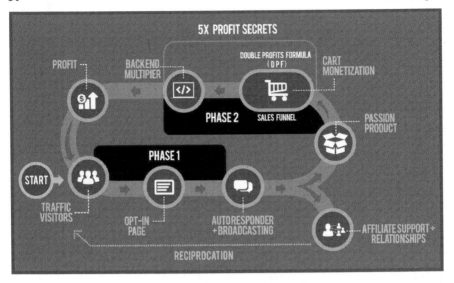

As you can see in this diagram, there are two phases to the Circle of Profit. Phase 1 is all about building an audience of fans: subscribers who trust you and look up to you as a qualified source for information. During this phase, you will grow your email reach by getting more and more people to give you their email address. You will nurture relationships with your new subscribers.

Most of all, you will start generating a healthy profit from these new subscribers. This way, your business can be profitable from Day One!

Phase 2 is about creating the $1 million. We take the monetization of your newfound influence to the next level. In this phase we focus on creating and promoting your own digital products (information products). These digital products could include ebooks, audios, videos, or even a combination of these.

This is where your profits are really going to explode! Phase 2 is the secret to quickly turning your passion into $1 million.

It really is as straightforward as that. Use the system to get some visitors to your website. Get them to give you their email address. Provide these new subscribers with value. Keep them happy. Present them the ability to buy great information products. Create profit. Then, just rinse and repeat.

You see, the more profit you create, the more you can invest to drive visitors back to your website. The more visitors you get, the bigger your email list. The bigger your email list, the more sales you get. The more sales you get, the more profits you make.

Do you see how that works now?

It forms *a circle!*

In the next chapter, I'm going to give you an overview of the different pieces that go into each phase. As you'll see, this model is not complicated. It all comes down to following the steps and focusing on providing value.

Now, let's dive into the key elements that you need to focus on if you want to start your business the fastest.

Chapter 7
The Key Elements to Starting Your Business

In just a few short minutes, you're about to be empowered with the quickest keys you need to actually start your business. We've had Profit Academy students start and actually have their first dollar in profit within just three days. The pace at which you see success is really up to you and how fast you execute.

Phase 1: Making Your First Profit

Phase 1 is all about **email marketing**. Here I am going to teach you how to start creating a profit by promoting products that already exist. You do not need to create anything new. All you need to do is send some emails to your new subscribers endorsing existing products.

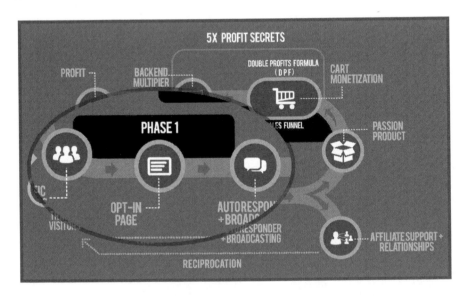

Using nothing but a simple link (we call it an *affiliate link*), you will begin to generate commissions (your share of a sale) that are as high as 75%. Yes, you can actually earn more than even the person who owns that product.

What Is a Subscriber Worth?

Assume you are in the business of teaching people how to invest in the market. Perhaps you have been able to use your investing strategies to completely change your life and now you want to help others.

Following the Phase 1 model, you begin to attract visitors to your one-page website and they start to share their email addresses with you. An email address (if treated properly) is worth a lot of money over your lifetime.

This email address is a true business asset.

A number very commonly accepted by information marketing experts is $1 per email. That means that if you can build an email list, by properly managing that list, you can generate a profit of $10,000 a month!

Remember, that number is not written in stone. In some niches, the number can be as low as 50 cents per email per month. In some niches, it can be as high as $5 per email per month.

Also, the longer you are a marketer, the better you get at it. The bigger your list, the better opportunities that come your way. Not to mention, when you launch Phase 2, your profit margins go up. All in all, your profits begin to grow (and your value per month, per lead goes up)!

To make the math easy, always focus on the $1 a month value. The magic of Phase 1 is that you can stop focusing on making money and simply focus on how many subscribers you have in your email list.

Next, let's quickly understand just how an email address is worth money to you. For this, we're going to need some math.

Are you ready to do some math?

How Does an Email List Translate Into Profits?

For this exercise to make sense, we have to make one key assumption: that you have built an email list of 10,000 subscribers.

Also—and remember, this is just an example—every piece of this math can and will change based on your list and even your individual emails.

Let's say you have 10,000 subscribers and you send an email to them. In that email you endorse a product as an affiliate (that means that someone else owns that product, and you just use a link to refer people to their site). Whenever a sale happens, you will get a commission (as high as 75%).

Now, you send an email.

Most likely, you should be able to get anywhere from 2% to 7% of your subscribers to click the link in the email. To keep math simple, let's assume 5%. That means that at least 5% of your 10,000 subscribers will click the link in the email (your affiliate link promoting a product); that equates to 500 clicks.

Now, typically, if the sales page is well done, I feel comfortable assuming you can get a 2% conversion (that means that 2% of the ones who click will buy the product). Again, remember, all these numbers change per promotion; some are better, some are worse. For this example, we're talking in terms of averages.

* * *

This would mean you get 10 sales (2% * 500 clicks). Now, let's assume the product costs $97 and you get 75% commission. Just on this promotion alone, you would generate more than $997 in sales.

At 75% commission, with just one email on one day, you would have earned $727.50.

That's over $700 in pure profit for just taking five minutes to write and send one email!

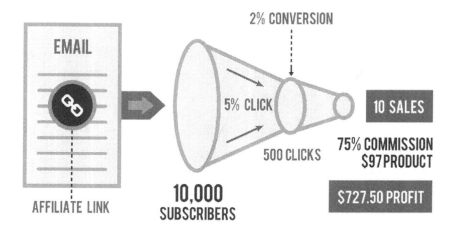

Even if you made HALF that, you'd be earning more than $10,000 a month.

NOTE: I want to emphasize that this is not a guarantee and a lot of factors can change these numbers, but I want you to just see how possible all of this is.

As you can tell from the math above, Phase 1 (*Building your Email List*) is incredibly important and profitable at the same time. Well, in Profit Academy we hold you by the hand and show you just how to master Phase 1 and start making profits right away. You can actually master Phase 1 very quickly with the right system. Many of our students are able to use Phase 1 to see profit within in less than a week.

The reason is that once you go through the right system, the circle of profit really only has three main parts:

1. Traffic
2. Your opt-in page
3. Your autoresponder

Let's break each of these down in detail.

#1 Part of Phase 1: Traffic

Imagine a quick example with me:

Let's say you open up a physical store near your house. Your store will never make any money unless people walk through the door, right? That is obviously the first step.

Well, the same thing applies to the Internet. When you use the Profit Academy system to quickly launch your online business, you will never stand a chance to make a profit unless you get people to visit your website. We call this **traffic**.

To paraphrase Kevin Costner's character in the movie *Field of Dreams,* "Build it and they will come." This is absolutely not true when it comes to your online business.

There are literally billions of pages on the Internet and most of them get no visitors; not even one. The ironic thing is that if you want traffic, it isn't hard at all! There is just a list of simple steps to follow; all you do is copy and paste.

One of the many miracles of the Internet is that getting traffic is *easy* and *inexpensive*. You don't have to spend thousands of dollars. You're not risking your life by buying a TV commercial or spending weeks trying to get a billboard put up. As a matter of fact, with the Internet, you can start with as little as $50 (*or even free*) and see your first profitable traffic in as little as 30 minutes.

The best part is that even if you don't want to invest $50 to start traffic, thanks to the Internet, you can get free traffic as well! The only thing free traffic requires is more of your time.

In chapter 11, I'm going to break down proven traffic-generating strategies that lead to immediate profit. Trust me: There's something for everyone and for any budget you can afford (even if your budget is $0).

Just look at all the options you have. It's amazing:

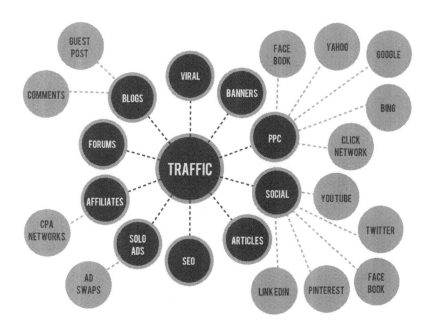

#2 Part of Phase 1: Your Opt-In Page

Let's go back to the example of building a store.

Obviously, if you go out and rent land, you would need to actually build the store, right? You would need shelves, desks, chairs, inventory, signs, lights, and so much more. This can end up costing you tens of thousands of dollars, if not more.

Nothing changes when you move to building an online business. You still need somewhere that people can actually go. However, there is one big difference.

You don't need thousands of dollars. You don't even need hundreds of dollars. Using the Profit Academy system, you can get your business presence online within a few clicks and for free!

All you need to start turning your passion into pure profits is a one-page website. That's it. We call these sites **opt-in pages**. You'll see why in just a minute.

The most amazing part is that these opt-in pages can be created without any technical experience. You never have to program or write even a single line of code. All you have to do is use our automated system and click a few buttons.

By the way, you never sell anything on these websites. At this point, you don't even have your own product. You've not spent any money or time creating anything.

Opt-in pages have only one purpose: to convince your site visitor to give you his or her email address and subscribe to your email list. In over 13 years of testing, I have found something very ironic. The simpler your opt-in pages are, the higher the conversion. If you try to get fancy and complicated, your conversions actually drop!

This is great news for you. This means that it's even easier than ever to start generating profits using Phase 1 of the Circle of Profit.

So when I say simple, what do I mean? Look at this example; this page was created using our *click-click technology*. It probably took about 7 minutes to create.

An Opt-in Page Example, Built Using the Profit Academy System:

* * *

This is it. This is how simple the page is. All we had to do to create this page was write the headline (the big bold words at the top). We chose some standard images that the system placed at the top and bottom. Then, we plugged in the title of our autoresponder (which is copy and paste) and *voilà* – we were in business!

How I Got 3,640 Subscribers in Three Days Using This Opt-In Page

I sent over 7,000 clicks to this page from various sources of traffic. My overall average conversion was 52%!

That means than more than 52% of the people who landed on this page gave me their email address; that is excellent!

In a matter of just three days I was able to build an email list of over 3,640.

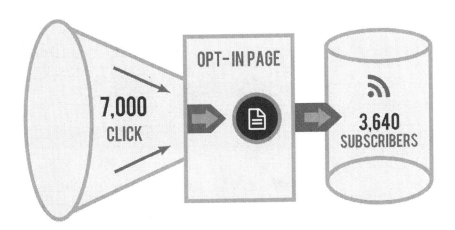

That page took me **seven minutes** to build. Then, I used our traffic strategies from the Profit Academy program to get 7,000 visitors in three days. Before I knew it, I was in business and generating a profit from Day One. How many businesses do you know that can launch and profit this fast?

---

* * *

#3 Part of Phase 1: The Autoresponder

The email addresses you collect on your opt-in page don't sit on your own computer. These email addresses actually automatically fly into a database through just a copy-and-paste line of code you use. This database of emails is called an **autoresponder**.

There are many third-party companies out there that manage this entire process for you. They give you one line of code that you copy and paste into your opt-in page. From there, the emails are automatically placed into your autoresponder. There are two major benefits to having an autoresponder.

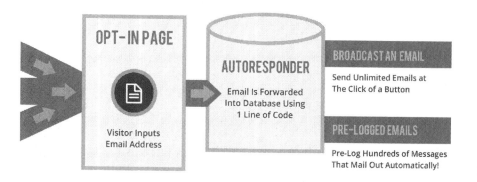

1. Sending thousands of emails in a matter of seconds.

You just type out the email once (just as you would to a friend) and then hit "send." Suddenly, the autoresponder system will automatically send thousands of emails. Hundreds, thousands, and even millions; it doesn't matter. The magical power of an autoresponder is that you can email them all with just the click of a button.

2. Automating and logging hundreds of messages ahead of time.

Talk about automation! With an autoresponder, you can pre-log as many emails as you want and the system will start sending your new subscribers daily emails, all on its own. The system automatically remembers which subscriber joined your list and on which day. According to their day, thousands of different subscribers can be getting thousands of different pre-logged emails everyday.

All this without your having to lift a finger!

These autoresponder services are available for a very small fee. There are tons of great ones out there. I plan on covering more on this topic in my free LiveCast training (*The Profit Workshop – www.FreeProfitWorkshop.com - please make sure to register for free*).

I will also share some amazing news: I have spent the last 18 months building my own autoresponder company that is specifically made with YOU in mind. We have created an amazing system that is more automated than any you have ever seen and is specifically built to facilitate the Profit Academy system. I will be offering everyone this system free for 60 Days. You can learn more about it on my Free Profit Workshop training at www.FreeProfitWorkshop.com.

In Chapter 9, I'm going to break down the secrets of how to use an autoresponder for maximum profits. I will show you three types of emails that automate the entire process.

I'm going to introduce you to Phase 2; this is the key phase that will help you turn your passion into $1 million. Just one reminder before we start: You will need to master Phase 1 before you go into Phase 2 if you want to build your business the fastest way possible. Remember, this is a circle. Each element of the circle feeds itself!

Phase 2: The Secret to Creating $1 Million

Phase 2 is all about turning your passion into $1 million. The best and fastest way to do this is by creating and promoting your own digital content products. If you do Phase 2 properly, you're going to see serious growth and fast profits. It's actually the secrets behind Phase 2 that took my business from about $300,000 a year to over $10 million a year.

There are two key elements to creating your first $1 million using Phase 2:

- **Your Passion Product**
- **Your $1 Million Funnel**

Let me introduce you to both really quickly:

* * *

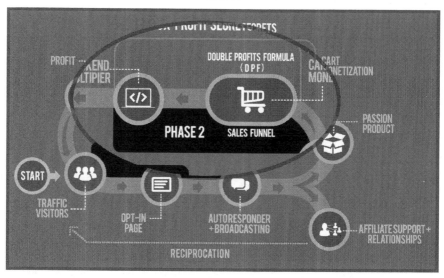

Your Passion Product

As long as you have access to information that can help others who share your passion (even if your main task were to aggregate the information into one place), you have what it takes to create a very successful digital product. You see, if you want to teach fitness, you do not need to be a certified trainer or nutritionist. Your credibility can come from many places; perhaps, you have lost a lot of weight yourself. Perhaps you partner with a friend who has the certifications. There are endless possibilities!

Remember that the whole magic of the Circle of Profit is that it allows you to build your business with a very small budget! If you join me in the Free Profit Workshop, I will share all the details about how I outsource most of my product creation. This way, I am busy traveling the world while others are creating highly valuable, amazing content for me (within an amazingly small budget).

Your $1 Million Funnel

The following took me at least three years to learn. However, after learning it, I became unstoppable. To really take your profits to the next level, you will hear me use a term many times: **funnel**.

A funnel is basically a group of products that are strategically sold, one by one, to existing customers. Here are some examples to help you understand.

You go to McDonald's and ask for a Big Mac. The cashier behind the register asks if you want fries with that. Then he asks you if you want a soda as well. You just took part in a small funnel! After you agree to become a customer by asking for a Big Mac, the company positions other beneficial and complimentary offers in front of you.

If you think about it, by just adding French fries and a soda to your order (only by asking you), McDonald's just doubled the size of your order. Imagine what that does to their revenue!

Time after time, in almost any kind of business, research has proven that a proper funnel can more than double the value of your customer almost instantly (right when they are checking out).

We'll get into more detail for that very soon.

In short, the basic goal of a funnel is to convince an existing customer to buy more products from the company; hence, increasing the lifetime customer value (and of course, profit).

In later chapters, I will show you actual examples of what a funnel looks like for a digital-product online business. This is one concept that absolutely changed my life!

Phases 1 and 2: Completing the Circle

The true power of the Circle of Profit lies in using Phase 1 and Phase 2 together. When built properly, the entire Profit Academy system can be automated using the Circle of Profit.

Always remember this:

Phase 1 helps you do a few key things:
- Start building your email list.
- Begin creating a fast profit from your business.
- Build an amazing relationship with your subscribers.

Phase 2 is when you really start to generate big profits:
- Building scale into your business.

- Generating profits that go into the millions.
- Being able to re-invest those profits.

The more each Phase grows, the more your profits skyrocket!

Now that we have the introduction of each Phase out of the way, let's dive into the details of Phase 1. It's time we started peeling back all the layers.

Time to rock and roll!

Chapter 8
Building Your Audience

Phase one of the Circle of Profit is all about building an audience of fans. The larger your audience, the more sales you make. The more passionate they are about you and your message, the more sales you'll make. The more sales you make, the larger you can afford to grow your audience (by re-investing in getting more traffic).

In order to get new fans to opt-in to your email list, you need to direct them to something called an *opt-in page*. This is where you basically bribe them with a free offer in exchange for their email address.

The best part is that it is very easy to make this opt-in page. It just takes a few clicks (especially if you use the technology that we use in the Profit Academy system). Remember, the simpler your opt-in page, the better your conversions will be (so this works in your favor).

Remember this example?

* * *

This simple page took me seven minutes to create. It converts at over 52%. I was able to launch a business in the fitness niche in less than one day. The entire key to this business is my opt-in page.

Without an opt-in page, you have no business.

Now, let's dive into the details of an opt-in page. If you want to create a high conversion opt-in page, there are only three elements to focus on:

- The Headline
- The Free Gift
- The Opt-In Box

Let's break down the three elements of a successful opt-in page:

1. The Headline

The headline is the most important part of the opt-in page. No opt-in page will ever work without a very strong headline.

FREE REPORT: Lose 10% of your unwanted Body Fat in the NEXT 30 Days! FREE

The headline is also the first and most prominent thing you see when you come to an opt-in page. It's big, bold, and has a very convincing promise.

Just look at our example. Within seconds of seeing this page, you are given a very strong and intriguing promise. You are being enticed to get free information on how lose 10% of your body fat in just 30 days.

Just think about: If you're someone looking to lose weight, this headline would catch your attention almost instantly. That's why this page can convert at 52%!

Years of testing has proven that the number-one element of an opt-in page that makes all the difference is the headline. You can make the graphics as pretty as you want, but the results of pretty graphics will not come close to the results you get with even a small tweak to the headline.

When someone comes to your opt-in page, you have only a few seconds to grab them. Your headline should always be the main thing they read and the promise should be strong enough to stop them in their tracks.

2. The Free Gift

Decades of marketing research has proven over and over that the most powerful word in marketing is *free*. It does not matter what you're giving away; if it's free, people will line up around the block to get it! If you had to ask me to give you one word that is most responsible for building my $10 million a year passion business, it would be *free*.

Even to get someone to give you his or her email address, you have to be willing to offer something in return. Rarely will anyone want to give you something personal like their email address without getting something in return. Because of this, we simply use an opt-in page to offer a small bribe.

We offer to exchange amazing information for free if they give us their email address. In this example, we are offering to give them a free report. This report could just be a 10-20 page PDF file that takes us very little time to create. However, it is more than enough to convince someone to give you his or her email address.

In the Free Profit Workshop (*www.FreeProfitWorkshop.com*), I will share many other ideas with you on just how to use free gifts to increase your opt-in conversions. I will also share how I easily get these free gifts created. It has rarely taken me more than one day to put together an amazing valuable gift.

* * *

3. The Opt-In Box

The final part of the opt-in page is the actual box where the visitor inputs her or his email address. This box is the easiest part of the process. You simply take copy-and-paste code from your autoresponder company and paste it here.

However, remember, without this box, the visitor's email address will never make it to your database. I make it a goal to always make my opt-in boxes with some reinforcing text. I will take time to emphasize the free offer again and make sure I close the deal for sure.

Here's an example:

As I mentioned before, the opt-in box is created very easily. You just copy and paste a line of code. This code is given to you by whichever autoresponder company you choose.

Examples of Opt-in Pages

Let's check out some examples of very high-converting opt-in pages.

* * *

Capturing 10,113 Emails in 45 Days

This is an example from one of our Profit Academy students. This opt-in page is in the Law of Attraction niche. The design of this page was done using a simple template. The entire page took our student less than 60 minutes to create.

In this example, the student chose to invest about $60 with an outsourcer (using the same techniques I teach) and the entire process was automated. The student never touched any technology.

After the page was LIVE on the student's domain name, she took another two days to create her free gift. This free gift was positioned as a short course that could be downloaded in PDF format. The entire PDF was only 40 pages; however, all 40 pages have amazing content in them. The gift was also made completely by an outsource agent and the entire investment was only $150.

So far, in less than three days, this student had her opt-in page and her free course completely done for only $210.

* * *

For just $210, this student had taken her passion for the Law of Attraction and converted it into a lifelong business that will be full of profits.

After the opt-in page and the free gift were LIVE, she began to generate traffic (using just two of the many traffic sources we teach inside the Profit Academy program).

She used free traffic
She used email media (which requires a small investment)

All in all, this student generated more than 22,473 visitors to this one simple page!

After all was said and done, the opt-in page converted at 45% and the student generated more than 10,113 subscribers. The student made her first profit within her first seven days in business and today, she is generating over $6,000 a month in income.

This income alone allowed the student to quit her day job and now the student is 100% focused on her passion business. She is expecting her passion product to launch any day now. The minute her product launches, she should immediately see her income jump from $6,000 a month to most likely over $15,000 a month.

This is the power of a simple opt-in page!

Here's another example:

* * *

Making $14,955 in the First 30 Days

Here is another student of the Profit Academy program.

This student chose to focus on the power of affiliate marketing. Through what he learned inside Profit Academy, he decided to teach the same strategies to others who share their passion for online marketing.

This opt-in page is about as simple as it gets and it was built within 20 minutes. The opt-in page was 100% built using our automated technology and cost the student nothing to build.

Investment in opt-in page = $0

The free gift on this page is an audio recording the student produced himself. He took a microphone and his laptop. He sat down to outline the audio course for about two hours and then took another two hours to record it.

* * *

The free gift was done in four hours and was LIVE immediately after that.
Investment in Free gift = $0

Within just one day, this student had a LIVE business, ready to go!

Next, the student chose only one source of traffic, which is 100% free. He invested absolutely no money into traffic and built a list of 5,450 within the first 30 days.

I want to make a mention here that the student spent about fours a day on traffic generation strategies because he did not want to invest even a small amount of money. This is absolutely fine, but just remember, if you don't invest money, you need to be ready to invest time.

Then, 25 days into building this email list...

...this student had a chance to promote a very strong affiliate product where the commissions were very high. The product cost $997 and the commission was 50%. That means the student would earn $498.50 per sale!

Using some very specific promotional techniques, before the first 30 days ended, the student was able to sell 30 units of this $997 product.

At his given commission level, he had now earned $14,955 in his first 30 days. These are the kinds of results we hear about all the time!

Next, the student has already begun working on his passion product ; he should see his income multiply in the next 30 to 45 days!

Amazing, isn't it?

* * *

I will cover even more examples in my Free Profit Workshop. You're about to see the awesome power this system contains. All you need to do is make sure that you are registered to attend our Free Profit Workshop.

Just go to: www.FreeProfitWorkshop.com and register yourself right away.

Remember, we start with Workshop #1 on February 23rd at 8:00 p.m. Eastern time. Our Workshop #2 is on February 26th at 8:00 p.m. Eastern, and Workshop #3 will be on March 2nd at 8:00 p.m. Eastern. No matter what you do, make sure you are there for these!

Now that you understand just how powerful and simple opt-in pages are, let's move on to the next necessary step. You need to learn how to build an amazing relationship with your newly found audience.

Chapter 9
Talking To Your Audience

"Communication: the human connection is the key to personal and career success." – Paul J. Meyer

With the help of your new opt-in page, you should have new subscribers flying into your email list. That's wonderful, but it takes more than just that to start making a profit. These subscribers are going to have to turn into raving fans who look at you as authority and take your advice seriously enough to make purchasing decisions based on your advice.

That's where the profit comes in!

To turn subscribers into fans, you need to actually communicate with them. That means you need to send them emails.

This is precisely where your *email autoresponder* comes in.

The invention of the autoresponder revolutionized online marketing. It automates everything involved with setting up and maintaining your email list. With an autoresponder, you can send emails to your audience in two ways.

- Pre-logged emails (based around the date they join your list).
- Broadcasting, or sending an email to all your subscribers at once.

When you use pre-logged emails, you can schedule emails ahead of time and the autoresponder system will automatically begin sending your subscribers emails. You can assign an email (that you only type once in your life) to go out immediately after the subscriber joins. The next one can be scheduled for one day after. The next, two days after. You have no limits; you could even schedule out 10 years if you really wanted.

* * *

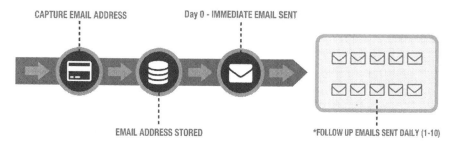

When using the broadcasting feature, you simply log in to your autoresponder. You type your email (there are three types of emails, which we discuss in the next section) and you hit *send*. Now, it does not matter if you have 500 subscribers or 50,000; that's all you have to do. Every person on your list will receive that email.

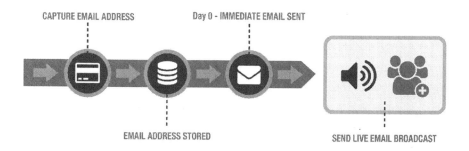

Personally, I would say that 95% of my wealth has been generated using the broadcasting feature. I use pre-logged emails for a very specific reason (discussed in the next section) and after that I turn my full focus to broadcasting .

Obviously, every autoresponder is different and they all have different features. Your ability to profit from your email list, then, depends on what features you are provided. Let's discuss the most common autoresponders in the market; I'll also share a secret with you that has been building for 18 months.

Autoresponders: Which One To Choose?

An autoresponder is a very key tool in your online business. It is also very difficult to switch once you are committed to one, so make your choice wisely right from the start.

Here are the three that you will hear about the most:

1. GetResponse

2. iContact

3. Aweber

These are the three most popular simply because of the features they offer, their pricing, and their frequency of use among the online business crowd. However, these are not the only ones available; there are many different autoresponder companies in the market and they all seem to have their own specialty or target customer.

My special announcement:

About two years ago, I was sitting around with three friends, all of them very acclaimed and brilliant online entrepreneurs. They all run passion businesses identical to what I'm teaching you (and make millions). We were all complaining about different automation and marketing features we found lacking among the existing autoresponders.

The more we spoke, the more we began to realize what a gaping hole there was in the email marketing world. If only someone could step up and fill that hole, we could all make so much more money That night we made a decision that led us to an amazing journey.

We all decided to come together and build our own autoresponder that was specifically built to support *online passion businesses.* We would build every feature that we ourselves dreamed of having and then make the service available to you!

The autoresponder is called **SendLane** and I will be revealing a lot more about it on the Free Profit Workshop that starts February 23rd.

I will also be giving away 90 days of SendLane for *free,* but only for our Profit Academy students. I can't wait to reveal more about this platform to you!

**How to Write Emails to Your Subscribers:
the Three Kinds of Emails**

There are three different types of emails you need to master. Each is very simple and my Profit Academy students get actual templates and examples to use. These three types of emails can be used for both the pre-logged emails and your broadcasting.

I have always found it more profitable to focus on broadcasting rather than the pre-logged autoresponder emails. I prefer to stay current with my list, talk about current events, and promote products (as an affiliate) with the most up-to-date sales message.

That doesn't mean that I do not use the pre-logged emails feature. Every scenario is of course different; however, I typically use the pre-logged emails in the autoresponder for the first 10 days of a customer's subscription just to introduce myself. I use the pre-logged emails to build a relationship with my subscriber; I use it as a tool for them to get to know me.

Of course, during the first 10 days, I also promote products to them; however, maybe not as hard as I will once I start broadcasting to them.

So, once a person gives me his or her email address:

Day 0 – Day 10 = pre-logged emails (autoresponder)

Day 11 – Lifetime = broadcasting

So, what are the three different types of emails that I recommend alternating? If you use a combination of these three, you will build a strong relationship with your list and you will begin to profit incredibly fast!

Remember, I recommend emailing your list as often as possible. I email my list at least once a day. I have known marketers who even email their list as often as three times a day (although I believe that might be overkill).

We have consistently found that students who email their list daily are far out performing the students who email their list only once a week. There is a common misconception that if you mail your list less frequently, they will pay more attention. This is simply not true and has been proven to be wrong many times.

The Three Emails

When you sit down to write an email to your list, keep a healthy balance and rotate between the following three:

1. **Content emails**
2. **Promotional emails**
3. **Relationship emails**

Here is a brief overview of each of the three (We will dive into the details soon.):

1. *Content Email*

This is your bread and butter. The key to making the Circle of Profit work is to give your customers a lot of value. That means you need to deliver good and helpful content to them. (There are many ways of getting this content; don't think you need to be brilliant or a published expert in the topic.)

Basically, your subscribers feel like they learn something new whenever they engage with you. They should have fun with your emails. Your subscriber should be excited to open your emails and the best way to get there is by writing a Content Email.

As you'll see later in the book and in the Free Profit Workshop (*www.FreeProfitWorkshop.com*), there are various types of easy content emails that you can put together in just minutes.

2. *Promotional Emails*

This is where the profit comes in. Typically, at least once a week, I recommend sending your subscribers a product that you believe will really help improve their lives. You can either promote your own products (discussed in the next section) or you can promote existing products as an affiliate (meaning you receive a commission from the sale).

Phase 1 focuses on promoting products as an affiliate. Phase 2 will focus on beginning to add your own products to the promotions.

I am a big fan of affiliate offers. The great thing about affiliate offers is that you never have to invest much time before you start generating profits. Many affiliate commissions are as high as 75% (you can actually earn more than the product owners themselves). All you need to do is find excellent products that others have created; get your personal affiliate link and endorse the product to your email list.

3. *Relationship Emails*

Let me ask you something. Who do you trust more: a friend or a stranger? The answer is easy; your friend! Likewise, you will get the best response from your list when they start seeing you more as a friend than some random person sending them emails.

I like to make my subscribers feel like they are a part of my life. My best students are the ones who take time to get personal with their list. They will send subscribers"inside" information about their worldly travels. They share personal stories with them, major moments in their life. Many even talk about their families!

These are all things we would do with our friends. When you get personal with your email list, it automatically triggers a part in the recipient's brain to regard you as a friend. After all, that's how the conversations go with their closest friends.

You see, the more personal you get with your list, the more trust you build with them. It becomes obvious so them that you have nothing to hide and that there is a real person behind that computer contacting them. The more trust you build with your email list, the more profits you will earn! Very shortly, I'm going to give you specific branding strategies that will allow you to get personal with your list with almost no effort and no time investment on your side.

"Anik, how was your gondola ride!"

I was recently in Las Vegas hosting a seminar. There were over 700 students there! All of these students are subscribers of mine and as I would soon learn, they are avid readers of the Emails I send out!

I was recently on my honeymoon. One of the places we visited was Venice. While I was traveling the World, we decided to run some promotions for a product I truly believe in. As we climbed onto the gondola ride in Venice, I had an ingenious idea.

* * *

"Why not shoot a video while on the ride and send it to my list?"

I made my poor wife hold the camera while I shot a three minute teaching everyone about a topic I was passionate about. Obviously, I started the video by sharing where I was, who I was with and what I was doing there.

I shot the video and I emailed it to my list. After that, I completely forgot about it!

Weeks later I was at this seminar in Las Vegas and I hear a student chasing me down from behind:

"Anik, how was your gondola ride?"

I freaked out. How did this student know I was on a gondola in Venice? I immediately remembered that I had shot the video and sent it to them. It didn't stop there.

During the event, I must have had at least twenty students bring up the gondola ride and far more asking *"can we meet your wife?"* I was being asked about where I went on my honeymoon and many other questions!

These were the types of questions my friends and family were asking me after the trip! I suddenly realized that by sharing these moments with my list, I was inviting them into my life. I was making them feel as if they were a part of my circle of family and friends!

Talk about trust. This is the true way to build your relationship with your list!

As we'll discuss later in this book, if you send out a nice mix of these three emails, you will keep your subscribers completely engaged. They will never grow blind to your emails because you will always keep it fresh. All of this combined is going to make a very sizeable impact on the amount of profits you generate from the list.

Trust me, I'm not a star writer or talented author. As I've mentioned, the only class I nearly failed in high school was writing. However, with the tips and tricks you'll learn later in this book and in the Free Profit Workshop, you're going to learn how to easily become a master author in the eyes of your subscribers, all by just writing a short email.

One of the most common hurdles I see students face is the fear of promoting a product to their list. We start to build such a strong relationship with our subscribers that we fear we might lose that relationship if we promote something to them. This couldn't be farther from the truth! Promoting or endorsing a product to your email list is one of the best ways to maintain and further build that relationship with your list.

Think about the last time you were at a mall and saw a huge sale at your favorite store. After you ran in and finished shopping, did you not call or text a few of your closest friends? Had you not called, would those friends not be a little miffed with you?

Better yet, think about the last time your friend saw you using something or buying a new product and then asked you how the experience was. If you loved the product, you most likely gave a raving review about it. The next day, that same friend goes out and purchases the same product. Did you feel bad then? If anything, you felt great and even proud!

This is why promoting a product to your list is actually doing them a service. You should never be shy to do it. Your subscribers will love you for it.

Let me show you a case study I recently conducted on my own subscribers. I wanted to test to see what they liked more: 100% pure content or a product endorsement.

I tracked two variables:
1. Open Rate – the percentage of my list who opened my email.
2. Click Rate – the percentage of my list who clicked a link in my email.

The results were amazing. I found that my list was far more engaged when I was sending a product recommendation than they were when I asked them to go to my blog to watch a free video.

I have since repeated this test three times and found the same results!

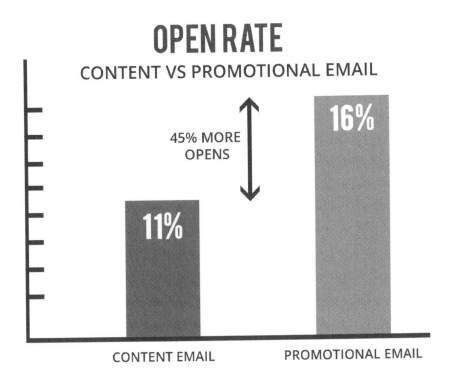

OPEN RATE
CONTENT VS PROMOTIONAL EMAIL

45% MORE OPENS

16%

11%

CONTENT EMAIL

PROMOTIONAL EMAIL

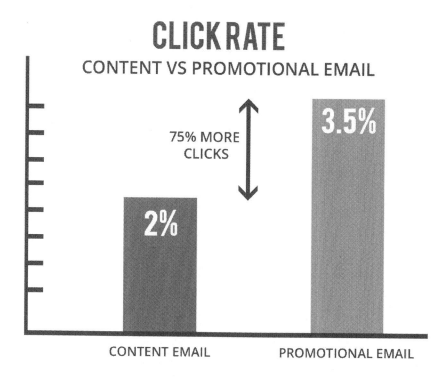

Moral of the story: Don't be afraid to promote a product to your subscribers. Don't be afraid to make some money!

Chapter 10
Monetizing Your Audience

"If you build a great experience, customers tell each other about that.
Word of mouth is very powerful." – Jeff Bezos

Starting to Make Money

If you focus on…
1. Delivering value to your email list;
2. Using a mix of the three email types in the previous chapter; and
3. Promoting and endorsing good products for them to buy,

… you should be in perfect shape to start monetizing your list (making money from your email list). After all, as we discovered in our case studies, once your subscribers trust you and become a raving fan, they actually want and prefer you to recommend products to them.

If you follow the guidelines in this chapter, there's no reason you can't start generating income from your list within days of Phase 1 going LIVE. As we proved to you before, Phase 1 can be LIVE very quickly. Many of my students follow the Profit Academy blueprint to go LIVE within just 3 days.

Unlike any other business model in the world (when online or offline), using the Circle of Profit, you never have to wait months or invest thousands of dollars to start seeing money coming in. You never have to knock down the doors of banks hoping for a loan or bicker with a venture capitalist to raise money. Your new start-up can be profitable within a matter of days!

Not only are you in profit fast, but the entire time you are immersed in your passion. There is truly no business model in this world that comes even close to offering this kind of freedom.

I do want to point out one thing, though. This is not some crazy get-rich-quick scheme. I can actually promise you that you are not going to become a multi-millionaire overnight. Let's face it; that kind of promise (no matter who makes it) is completely impossible. My promise to you is that you will start generating profits *almost immediately*. You can reach $10,000 a month within a matter of just weeks (if you follow the the system exactly). Most of all, you are learning a lifelong system that will stand the test of any economy.

Of course, as you finish building your entire Circle of Profit, you will be completely empowered to turn your passion into $1 million. However, there is a process involved and you have to do every step of it. There will be hard days and there will be obstacles; that is guaranteed. But, the best part is that if you choose to work with the Profit Academy team, we will be here to hold your hand through the entire process.

You absolutely can and will turn your passion into $1 million —just not overnight and not without implementing every step in the Circle of Profit.

The Two Quickest Ways to Generate Profits From Day One

Case Study: Keith Marks

Keith was a police officer for 10 years. He left that career and started his own business building ponds and waterfalls. However, when the economy crashed, his business took a hit, and Keith was back to Square One.

Keith saw Internet marketing as an opportunity to once again create his own business. He invested in multiple programs, some of which were helpful and others that were not so helpful.

Keith first saw Anik on stage in Denver. He was impressed with Anik and signed up for Anik's Profit Academy. Unlike he had in other courses, this time Keith took away clear, actionable steps to take his online business to the next level.

Now Keith is finally on his way to creating the liberating, profitable business he's always wanted.

As we discussed earlier, the most profitable way to monetize your email list is to actually create and promote your own passion product. However, that will take a few weeks to build. Also, you need to first take your time to learn how it's all done. The next section of this book is all about how you can create your own products for maximum profit.

However, why should we wait all that time. Let's start making some money right away using other people's products and promoting them as an affiliate.

When promoting products as an affiliate, there are two key ways to start making money very quickly:

1. The Thank-You Page (TYP) Method
2. Affiliate Marketing: using broadcasts to promote existing products in exchange for a commission

Quick Profit Strategy #1: The TYP Method

What if I told you that you could immediately start generating money from your list the second someone subscribes to your newsletter? That means that the instant someone gives you an email address, you can actually create a profit. I call this method the Thank-You Page, or **TYP Method**. This method alone has changed the lives of countless students of mine.

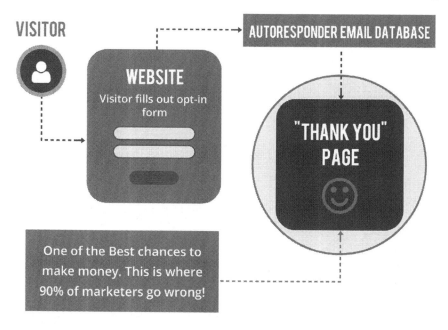

When someone enters an email address into your opt-in page, two things happen:

1. The email is sent to an autoresponder and stored inside a database.

2. The person is re-directed to a "Thank You" page.

It's called a Thank You Page because typically, the page would thank someone for subscribing to the newsletter. About 90% of the time, it is a dead white page with a simple thank-you message. Every time I see this, it breaks my heart because I can only imagine how much money that person is losing.

This is seriously one of the biggest mistakes made on the Internet! Let me describe why.

Anyone would agree that the best time to sell something is when you have someone's attention. Here are two scenarios; try to imagine them:

A. Someone is doing a regular daily check of her email and she suddenly sees a small advertisement and clicks it. She passively clicks the ad to see what it is about.

B. Someone goes to your website, likes your first free offer and decides to give you his email address. He's eager to get the information you promised so as soon as he puts his email address in, he is eager to see what is on the other page.

I think it goes without saying that you will have a much easier time selling someone in scenario B. The bottom line is that the person is paying attention to you! He has already said YES and shown that he trusts you. He is also fully engaged at that moment. However, still so many marketers don't know that they can control the look and feel of the TYP and they leave it like this boring standard one:

Thanks for signing up!

The Free Report we promised you will be sent to your inbox shortly.

While you wait for your materials to arrive via email, we recommend you to **click continue below to learn more about us and what it can do for your business.**

MAIL

Legal Information

The thank-you page is the most wasted real estate on the Internet. Even the simplest of autoresponder companies allows you to just copy and paste any link you want into the thank-you field. That means that you can direct your new subscriber to any page of your choice. You don't have to keep their standard boring thank you page!

I've figured out that even if you simply copy and paste an affiliate link into the thank-you field, you will make much more money than using the typical standard page. That is why I call this strategy the *TYP Method*.

There are two ways to deploy the TYP Method:

1. Forward the new subscriber directly to an affiliate offer (someone else's product sales message).

2. Forward the new subscriber to your own offer.

Assuming we are still in the middle of Phase 1, I will assume we are going to use strategy #1 and use affiliate offers. What you have to do is very simple!

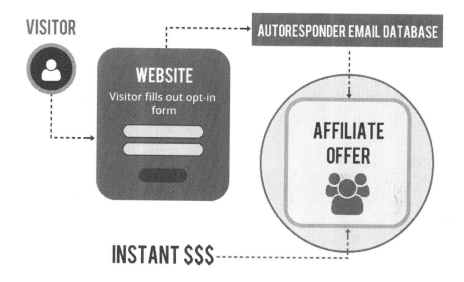

You have to find your affiliate link for a good product with a strong marketing message. I will use *Clickbank.com* as an example. Clickbank is a marketplace for online (educational) products that you can instantly promote and earn up to 75% commission. This is an excellent company that always pays on time and is trustworthy.

You will go to Clickbank and get your own link, which takes about 30 seconds. This link allows Clickbank to track every visitor you send to the website. If anyone buys from them after having clicked your link, you automatically get a commission (a percentage of the total sale – as high as 75%).

There are many other companies like Clickbank. The term *affiliate link* is common for all of them. For the sake of this example, I will use Clickbank.com

Here's what your affiliate link looks like (a long, technical looking URL):

ClickBank pays you 75.0% when you sell MANIMIR's product. To refer a customer send them to this domain name:

http://0d28d4o8pmrko5z7efn8mpbkbx.hop.clickbank.net/

Copy the following HopLink HTML code and add it to your web page:

`<a href="http://0d28d4o8pmrko5z7efn8mpbkbx.hop.clickbank.net/" target="_top">Click Here!</a>`

WARNING: *Due to the possibility of transcription errors, we recommend copying the HopLink from this page instead of typing it manually. To copy the HopLink, click on the text of the HopLink and either right click and select copy or hit Ctrl-C.*

This HopLink has been encrypted by HopLink Shield. It represents an encrypted version of the traditional HopLink format of *http://affiliate.vendor.hop.clickbank.net.*

You don't need to understand anything else. Just copy that link and paste it in the "thank you URL" field inside your autoresponder. You're officially done! Now, when someone subscribes to your list, she or he will be directed to the affiliate offer and tracked to you. Some of your new subscribers will choose to make a purchase right away. When they do, you will make a sizeable commission!

The TYP Method: Segway Page

We have developed a neat technology that sits in between your opt-in page and the affiliate offer. When our students started implementing the TYP Method in the thousands, we noticed a small issue developing.

Some subscribers started complaining that they were promised a free report but instead taken to a "sales pitch." They felt that they never got the free report (when in reality the Free report had been emailed to them all along*)*. They just didn't know to check their email; no one told them.

Because of that, we created a technology that will allow you to create a **segway page** that the visitor lands on right after they subscribe. The page has a countdown timer on it and a message that says something like:

"Your Free Report Is Being Emailed to You – Please Wait to Watch This Amazing Free Video…"

Suddenly we found that no one was complaining any more and we also had no changes in our commissions! We decided to make this even easier for you. If you want to learn how you can get your hands on this technology, make sure to join us in our Free Profit Workshop training series (www.FreeProfitWorkshop.com). It's Free to save a seat for the LIVE training or even to watch the replay!

Quick Profit Strategy #2:
Affiliate Marketing Through Broadcasting

As I mentioned in the previous chapter, you want to make sure you send out promotional emails. Your list is more active when you actually send product endorsements. This ends up being a win-win for you!

As I like to spend the first 10 days leaving the new subscriber in the autoresponder series, my most active broadcasting starts on Day 11. I want to note, though, that I also promote and endorse products during my first 10 days. Even when I am building a relationship with my list (using the pre-logged messages for the first 10 days), I still participate in product endorsements.

However, my most active affiliate promotions begin on Day 11 using broadcasts. I will find a good product that I believe can really help my subscribers and that has a great sales message (for high sales conversion) and I will grab myself an affiliate link for it.

Then, I will follow the simple template that we provide and write out two or three emails endorsing the product. I log into my autoresponder and log the broadcasts to go out over a period of three to four days.

Remember, I like to send my list an email every day. I don't *promote* to them everyday, but usually I will follow a schedule like this one. (This is just an example and can be altered as you wish.):

Broadcasting Schedule for One Week:
- o   Monday = General Content Email (prepare for the topic of the promotions)
- o   Tuesday = Promotional Email #1
- o   Wednesday = Promotional Email #2
- o   Thursday = Break
- o   Friday = Promotional Email #3
- o   Saturday = Content or Relationship Building
- o   Sunday = Break

No matter what, always keep the word *value*. Even when you're promoting affiliate offers or using the TYP Method, you should only be endorsing products that you believe in and know will add value to your subscriber. The easiest way to kill your email list and ruin your relationship is by endorsing a bad product solely for the purposes of making the most money. Trust me; you cannot do that for very long without paying the ultimate price!

We now have an opt-in page ready to go. We have the TYP Method in place so we can make money right away. We're even ready to communicate with our list as soon as we start getting subscribers.

It's now time to go out and find subscribers! It's time we started getting people to visit our new opt-in page.

A recent student was amazed by the simplicity of the system and how it generated traffic and subscribers!

Nick started at zero and built his list to over 10,000 subscribers in a matter of weeks, simply by following a few simple steps he learned in the program.

In Nick's own words "This is freakin' fantastic, a bit scary at the edge of my comfort zone, but starting to really believe. ACTION is the silver bullet!

– Nick Matthews, UK

Chapter 11
Attracting Your Audience

"Build it and they will come." - paraphrased from the
film *Field of Dreams*

In the last few chapters, you have learned about how Phase 1
works. You now know what an opt-in page is. You're now ready to
start making money by promoting other people's products. You have
almost everything you need, but you are missing one critical piece:
You need to get people to your opt-in page so they can give you their
email address.

The truth is that you can have the most amazing opt-in page
in the world, but if nobody is visiting that page, you'll never make a
penny. This is where the topic of *traffic* comes in. Traffic refers to
the people who are visiting your website.

As I mentioned earlier, one of the many miracles of the
Internet is that getting traffic is *easy* and *inexpensive*. You can start
getting traffic within minutes (for a tiny budget) from websites like
Google, Facebook, Bing, and many more. My company has even
developed one of the fastest growing traffic networks in 2014. It has
just officially launched!

All in all, getting traffic to your website has become easy.
Many of our students begin to consistently attract 1,000+ visitors a
day to their new opt-in pages, all using the traffic strategies we teach.

Remember: You can get traffic on even the smallest
shoestring budget and in many cases, you can even get traffic to your
opt-in page for free. I'll introduce you to both worlds and you can
choose from there.

If you want targeted traffic fast, you will need a tiny budget to
invest in getting that traffic. If you want only free traffic, then you
will need to invest time in order to get it. This is the traffic trade-off
when you're just getting started: money versus time. If you have
money to invest in your new business, you can get quick results by
investing even just a few hundred dollars. If you're using the TYP

Method, you will typically get a large portion of that investment back immediately anyway; the remainder is usually back in your pocket before the first 30 days are even up!

If you don't want to invest any money, then you need to be prepared to spend time using content to fuel your marketing. When you use content to fuel your marketing, it of course requires the time to create that content. Free traffic employs the use of sources such as forums, blogs, and other online communities in your niche.

There are many places where you can find traffic for your opt-in page. This diagram gives you a taste of all the options you have when it comes to traffic:

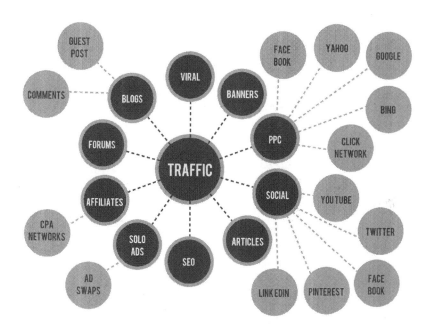

We're going to discuss many of these in the Free Profit Workshop (www.FreeProfitWorkshop.com). I'm also going to go into some great detail on each of them during the Profit Academy training. (Doors open on February 23).

However, I want to help get you started right away. I'm going to give you three sources of traffic that you should focus on when you're just beginning. As you can tell from the diagram above, there are many places to go. If you try to do too much at once, you're going to quickly get lost in the mess. This is why we recommend our students start with either one of the following three choices. The first two require a small investment to start and the third one is free.

Fast Traffic Option #1: Email Media

Email media is by far the best source of investment traffic for you to start building your email list. This traffic is fast, highly targeted and virtually guaranteed to work. Email media works in a similar way to buying an advertising slot on a TV station or a radio station. However, instead of buying a 30 second commercial, you are buying a dedicated email drop.

Let me explain:

Bob has an email list of 100,000 subscribers who are all interested in personal development. Bob sends out daily emails with great content and occasional promotions.

Many people in Bob's position will also offer email advertising to their list. The most common term is *solo ad*. This is when Bob will send an email to his list that is 100% written by you. The only content in that email will be whatever you write.

Of course, you will then attach a link in that email that his subscribers can click. In the case of the Circle of Profit model, we teach you to make sure that link is going to your own opt-in page.

Suddenly now, you begin to get subscribers from Bob's email list joining your email list. Bob can also charge you in two ways:

1.   A set price (flat fee) to send out the email.

2.   A fee per number of clicks they send to you.

Here's a quick diagram that really explains how the traffic source works:

* * *

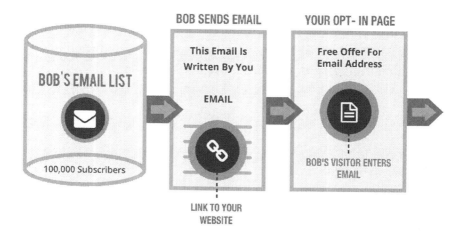

Depending on what target niche you are in, you can get traffic for as little as $.30 a click to as high as $1.50 a click. Everything depends on the source, the niche, and many other things.

The reason why solo ads are such a good source of traffic is that your opt-in page is being promoted to people who are highly targeted. They are already subscribed to an email list similar to yours and have proven that they open those emails and also click the links! You're getting a very targeted customer. Email media also tends to be less expensive than many sources of traffic (when comparing how targeted the traffic is).

In 2014, many of our students were struggling to find vendors from whom to buy email media. It was a very tedious and manual process. To better server our student community, we created a platform called **Clickonomy**.

The best place to buy email media now is Clickonomy (www.clickonomy.com). It is an exciting new marketplace that is all about selling and buying email media. Whether you're just starting your email list or already have a well-developed one, Clickonomy is the best place to quickly find great traffic sources. You can buy the traffic right on Clickonomy and use our entire network to protect your investment. We can even turn around and start selling clicks and earning an income!

We have thousands of students already using Clickonomy.

Clickonomy is absolutely free to join and there are traffic sources inside that apply to many niches. Clickonomy is growing every day; we are attracting new traffic vendors that cover a wide range of niches. Before you ever make even a dollar in investment, you get a chance to read tons of reviews and see what the community is saying about that seller.

Furthermore, any investment you make is safe in an escrow account and the entire Clickonomy team is consistently watching for fraud. If anything bad happens, your funds will be safe with us and returned right back to you!

I believe every serious list owner should be on Clickonomy. There's simply no better resource for driving paid traffic to your list, especially if you're getting your business off the ground. As soon as you get your opt-in page up, head over to Clickonomy, register your free account and start exploring!

Fast Traffic Option #2: Facebook Ads

Learn how one of our students used Facebook to jumpstart his business:

Over a billion people use Facebook to connect with their friends, favorite brands, and more. That's why Facebook is one of the major platforms to utilize in your business.

I use Facebook daily in my own business. The platform has been a major customer acquisition strategy for the past two years. I used Facebook advertising to build a 10,000+ subscriber list in only a few months with a very small investment and the teachings inside the Profit Academy program.

I also used Facebook to create a 33,000+ community of highly engaged members in my own niche. Within three months I had paid for all my advertising expenses and now I am in the GREEN, plus I own a very sizable list and a large community that I can monetize for as long as I want!

Facebook advertising is unique, unlike most online advertising that reaches only 38% of its intended audience. Facebook's average is 89%. So essentially your business gets more exposure and more value from every ad.

In my opinion, Facebook is the New Google and if you haven't used it yet, I recommend that you start now. More than anything, if you haven't started using The Circle of Profit, you better start using that now too!

Zane Baker

There are a few things I absolutely love about getting traffic from Facebook:
1. No matter what niche you're in, Facebook has targeted traffic.
2. You can start generating traffic for as little as $50 (*or even less*).
3. You can get your targeting very specific!
4. If done right, the traffic can be very inexpensive!

Facebook now has over *1.23 billion* users. If Facebook were a country, it would be the third largest in the world. This is why I say that no matter what topic you are building a list on, Facebook has millions of people you can quickly target. Facebook also has an impeccable and easy to use advertising system. It's one of the simplest ones I have ever seen.

After logging in and initiating your advertising account (which takes 30 seconds), you have to simply fill out one page. On this page, you specify who you want to target and what you are willing to spend. That's it.

Facebook will then review your ad and your landing page. They have been known to approve ads in as little as 15 minutes or a maximum of 12 hours (from what I have seen).

Here is what you are counting on when you advertise with

Facebook:

You give Facebook a few targeting qualifications. These qualifications tell Facebook who your target customer is and they will show your advertisement only to those people. Let's again assume that your ideal target visitor is represented by Bob.

Bob would log into Facebook at any time to simply check what is happening in his social world. As he scrolls through pages and pages of newsfeeds and pictures, he will start seeing small ads in various places.

Suddenly, one catches his eye. Bob finds the promise in the advertisement and clicks the ad. Bob has now landed on your opt-in page!

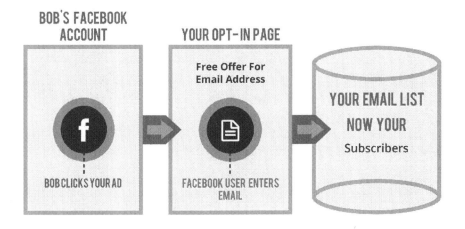

All in all, Facebook ads might not be as straightforward as email media (*solo ads*), but Facebook is a great traffic to consider adding as soon as you can. Facebook is also very scalable from one place.

Inside the Profit Academy training, we have hired professional Facebook advertising experts to be your personal coaches. They will show you every great secret about Facebook. These experts typically charge $1,000 an hour or more. However, they will be available to train all our Profit Academy students for free.

Profit Academy will be very limited and we will review who

qualifies for admission on the LIVE Free Profit Workshop training that I lead.

Fast Traffic Option #3: Forum Commenting

If you are looking for a 100% free source of traffic, your best bet is to find a forum related to your topic and become a contributor. It's pretty straightforward: Contribute to whatever discussion is going on, and gently promote your opt-in page at the same time. However, you never want to promote your opt-in page in the actual post; that is rarely allowed in a community.

In most forums all you to have is a static signature file below every post you enter. Believe it or not, these signatures are read pretty closely. I remember doing a test once and finding that with a strongly written signature file, I was able to get close to 20% of those who opened the discussion thread to click my link!

Many of the big forums will easily generate 2,000+ views on a good topic you post. If you can grab 20% of that 2,000, you would be getting over 400 free views per topic that you start on the forum. Imagine if you can start two new topics a day: That is a potential of getting 800+ visitors a day to your website for free, and for just participating in an online community.

Remember to always focus on providing value and never coming across as a spammer.

Here's how forum marketing works:

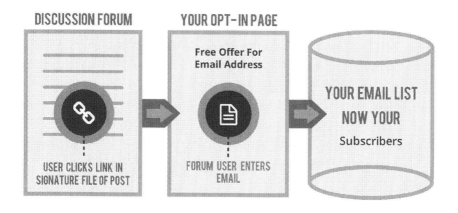

DISCUSSION FORUM

YOUR OPT-IN PAGE

Free Offer For
Email Address

YOUR EMAIL LIST
NOW YOUR
Subscribers

USER CLICKS LINK IN
SIGNATURE FILE OF POST

FORUM USER ENTERS
EMAIL

Let's pick on Bob again. Let's say Bob is cruising around a watch forum because he is a big fan of watches. He has a tendency to participate in a lot of the discussions and checks the forum at least once a day.

Suddenly, he sees a topic that really interests him and he opens it to start reading and learning more. The first post he sees is by you. You've written a detailed post explaining something. Bob is intrigued by your content so he reads it all the way through. As he is finishing your post, he sees your signature file at the bottom:

The signature says your name, your website and a catchy phase like *"Learn How To Get Designer Watches For 50% Off – Free Report!"*

Bob is intrigued and clicks the link. He finds himself at your opt-in page and decides to share his email address with you to get his free report. This is precisely how we get free traffic using forums!

It's a very powerful traffic strategy. Actually, forum marketing is how I made my first $10,000 on the Internet.

The Truth Behind My First $10,000 Online

I still remember back in February 2002 when I first started trying to make money on line. I got addicted. I would spend hours and hours studying and trying. I had two offices.

I was just 19 years old. I was so addicted that I started skipping classes and even went days without any sleep. In those days, I had only one dream: Make $10,000 a month on my own. I was tortured by the thought of "doing what everyone does." The thought of having a boring job tormented me, so I set out on a road of my own.

I wanted to pave my own path, control my own destiny. But the road wasn't easy. Many times, I felt like quitting. I kept having this nagging feeling that getting a job was just so much easier and less stressful. But, somehow, I refused to give up. I could feel the dream. I felt like I could see it; it was near! I struggled and banged my head against a wall for over 18 months looking for the secret key to online success.

• I bought products.
• I bought software.
• I went to workshops.
• I went to seminars.
• I hired coaches.

I did it all. The whole nine yards. But for 18 months, I had nothing to show for it. Not a dime. Then, suddenly, one day, it clicked. I spent the entire night working. I must have worked for 24 hours straight before I literally passed out at my computer, my head on the keyboard. I woke up to the moment of truth.

This was it. I was on my last nerve. I had made a decision the night before. That was the day that my life would change forever. "If this doesn't work…I quit and I'm getting a J.O.B." I still remember the feeling when I logged onto my computer. My heart plummeted to my stomach. Then I rubbed my eyes. I checked again just to make sure I wasn't dreaming.

"Have I finally done it? Is this REAL?"

I had earned $540 in 10 hours, and all that while I SLEPT! I still cannot explain the feeling I had when I saw that. It was priceless. I still get goose bumps when I think about it. It was one of the greatest days of my life. I knew it. I had finally cracked the code. Now, all I had to do was "rinse and repeat."

Thirty days later, I had earned over $10,000.

Oh…and how did I drive all my traffic that month? Free traffic from forums!

Anik

There really isn't much else to say about this source of traffic other than you need to put in a lot of time to get good results. Commit to spending at least 30 minutes a day commenting on forums in your niche. If you are consistent, you should see a steady stream of traffic coming to your opt-in page.

These three sources of traffic are a great start, but this is a tip of the iceberg. In the official Profit Academy training, we got into great details on many traffic sources. You will be able to generate more traffic than you can ever imagine!

Chapter 12
Become A True Authority

"Become an expert in your field and success will follow."
– Robert Kihlstrom

You now have everything you need to start building your list of raving fans and even to start making your first money! You know how to create a killer opt-in page that converts. You know how to get as much traffic as your heart desires (to build your list). Now, you also know how to communicate with your new email list in such a way that builds a tremendous relationship with your subscribers.

If you really want to see success fast, stop thinking about money and start thinking about subscribers. I've consistently found (no matter what niches I enter) that each subscriber on my mailing list is worth at least $1 to $3 a month in revenue. That means if I have a list of 10,000 and I manage it properly, I should be able to generate at least $10,000 to $30,000 a month!

This means you have a simple profit formula: The more subscribers you add, the more money you make. It becomes a wonderful circle of profit: new subscribers lead to more profit, which gives you more money to buy new subscribers, which leads to even more profit.

While you are using the Circle of Profit to start and grow your business, there's an important word you want to keep in mind as we go into Phase 2: **Branding**.

Branding is one of those terms you hear about all the time, but few rarely explain why it is important. We have talked a lot about *relationship building* during Phase 1. There is a very specific reason for this. We are training your list to look upon you as an authority. Your subscriber needs to feel that any time she needs help in a specific niche, you are the person to talk to.

The more he looks at you as an authority, the stronger your business will be and the more profit you will generate. This is especially true as you enter Phase 2 of the business-building process.

Throughout Phase 1, along with Phase 2 for that matter, it is important to *always* be mindful of your brand, what products you are promoting, what messages you are sending out, and what you are displaying about yourself to your subscribers.

That's why, before you send out an email, ask yourself, "Is this adding to the strength of my brand, or is it taking away from it?" Sometimes I have to say no to promoting a certain product (even if it's a great product) because I believe that endorsing it will impact my brand negatively.

I always review the sales material used. I always review the content and I also do my background search on the person who is teaching any course. I take responsibility for what I am sending to my subscribers because they trust me. If there is even one small thing that could hurt my brand, either I am transparent with my list about it or I just do not promote the product.

Beyond the types of emails you send, there are wonderful tools out there to make it even easier to create and strengthen your brand as an authority to your subscribers. Remember, the reason I am emphasizing *brand* so much is that soon you are going to be selling your own products. The stronger your brand in the market, the easier it will be to sell your product and to also get others to promote your product for you.

As you get ready to build out Phase 2 of your business, you will want to look into having a few types of properties online to help you boost your brand and get your message out.
- **Your own blog**
- **Your own YouTube channel** (Videos are an amazing way to build a relationship and brand.)
- **A Facebook page**
- **A Twitter account**

You do not need to use every one of these, but the more you use, the better your results will be. Personally, I have my own blog, an active YouTube channel and also a very active Facebook page with nearly 100,000 followers. However, to this day I've never become interested in Twitter. When it comes to building your own brand, you have full say on what you want to do. I am just here to give you some ideas.

This is where Phase 1 connects with Phase 2. If you've done your work in Phase 1 and built a strong list with whom you have a strong relationship, you are ready to move into Phase 2!

In Phase 2, we are going to plunge into the first major step of turning your passion into $1 million. It's time you really build your own business and see that 500% increase in your profit.

Are you excited? Let's turn the page and keep going!

Section 3

Generating $1 Million & Becoming an Authority

Chapter 13
The Hidden Key—Digital Products

"Think big and don't listen to people who tell you it can't be done.
Life's too short to think small." – Tim Ferris

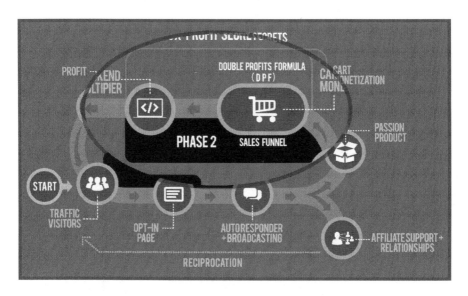

In this section, we're going to explore Phase 2. This is the phase where it becomes pretty simple to start making multiple six or seven figures. Our goal is simple: We're going to position you to turn your passion into $1 million. I use this phase in my business, over and over. The knowledge here is the groundwork to how I've created a $10-million-a-year business.

I still work from my home office and travel the world about 70% of the time. Can you imagine being able to scale your business to $10 million a year while living the life of your dreams?

It's completely possible through the world of digital products.

I'm not the only one who has used digital products to create millions and millions of dollars on line. There are thousands of other people who have done the same.

Here's how it works. In Phase 1, you built an email list, full of subscribers who trust you and have built a relationship with you. You are now able to monetize that relationship immediately by promoting other people's products as an affiliate. You simply collect a commission on every sale you refer.

This is the fastest way to start making money because you don't have to invest any time in making your own product. That's the benefit of using affiliate marketing.

However, there is a small disadvantage as well.

As an affiliate, you have a slight glass ceiling on what you can earn. You earn money only when you actively promote a product. You will never make more than 50% or 75% of the sale. There is a reason that product owners are willing to give an affiliate such high commissions; it's because they know they generate a lot more money from that customer during the lifetime of the customer.

However, as an affiliate, you don't get to participate in those profits.

Phase 1 is a great vehicle to allow you to start making money fast and to quit your job. However, if you want to start making millions, you're going to need to become the product owner. You're going to want to be in a situation where other affiliates are promoting *your* products!

The Power of Digital Products

Creating and launching your own product allows you to add unlimited scale to your business. Here are a few enormous benefits:

1. You immediately begin to make 100%, rather than only 50% or 75%.
2. You get other affiliates to promote your product and build scale into your business!
3. You build out a strong "back end" to make far more profits in the lifetime of a customer (more on this later in this book).
4. You build a true asset that has a value in the market. This product and the business behind it can be sold!

With your own product, you get full control over your future.

Some students are frightened by the prospect of creating their own digital products because they feel incapable or do not feel they have expert knowledge. The entire process can actually even be outsourced. I will give you a formula that you can use over and over. This formula can take absolutely anyone in the world and suddenly empower them to create an internationally best-selling product!

On the Internet, generating profits always comes down to two major factors:

- **Traffic** (people coming to your website)
- **Conversion** (how many of those visitors become customers)

Conversion is the easy part because it can be taught and tested. However, most marketers struggle when it comes to generating visitors to their website (traffic). Again, having your own digital product greatly helps solve this problem as well!

The forms of traffic available to you when you sell your own digital products suddenly explode and a completely new world of opportunity opens up!

That's the real magic here. You now have the ability to bring on other people who will sell your products for you. You don't have to buy this traffic; you never have to put even a dime at risk. You simply pay these affiliates only when they generate a profitable sale!

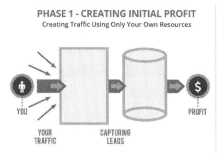

PHASE 1 - CREATING INITIAL PROFIT
Creating Traffic Using Only Your Own Resources

YOU — YOUR TRAFFIC — CAPTURING LEADS — PROFIT

PHASE 2 - USING SCALE TO CREATE MILLIONS
Using Affiliates To Create Unlimited Scale To Traffic

AFFILIATES — UNLIMITED FREE TRAFFIC — CAPTURING LEADS — PROFIT — GETTING IMMEDIATE SALES — PROFIT

In essence, you are now able to partner with an unlimited number of people who are themselves in the process of building Phase 1. Initially there was just one of you; now there can be hundreds. Imagine the amount your profit will multiply with just this one factor!

This is why the secret to turning your passion into $1 million lies in creating and marketing your own ***digital products***.

As the name implies, digital products are those that are hosted, sold, and delivered using the Internet. You never have any inventory, warehouse, or development costs. You can scale digital products to an unlimited level. You could sell 1,000 copies or 10 copies and your operational costs will remain largely the same (as opposed to when you have physical products that have to be produced, stored and delivered).

Examples of digital products include eBooks, audio recordings, and video courses. This book is an example of a digital product. You are reading it on your computer, tablet, phone, or e-reader. It's literally a digital file and nothing more. Whether five people read it or five million, my costs for delivering this book will barely change. (*Isn't that amazing?!*)

Examples of Digital Products

Digital books (PDF, Kindle, etc.)
Video courses
Webinar-based courses (delivered through live training)
Audio courses (MP3, podcasts, etc.)
Software (although our focus in this book is on informational products)
Multi-media (interactive games, and programs that educate)

The best digital products have a nice mix of many kinds of media. The course might have some written parts with video added to augment the training. The more kinds of media you add, the easier it is for your student to consume the content and the more valuable your product becomes. Everyone is different, so different kinds of products will appeal to different people; some like watching a video, whereas others prefer to read.

For example, my wife and I recently took the same course. I went through the entire course by reading only the PDF summaries of each video. I found this quicker and sufficient for what I needed. However, my wife never read a single PDF summary; she far preferred to watch all the videos.

Profit Academy: A Perfect Living Example

I practice what I preach :)

When you get a chance to log into the Profit Academy training, you will see that it is a purely digital product. However, we make use of many forms of multi-media to deliver the training to our students.

We have:

- Videos released every week
- PDF summaries of each video
- LIVE webinar training every week to supplement the video
- LIVE virtual workshops (run over the computer over weekends where we dive into detail on a certain topic for 2 days and bring in experts from around the world).
- LIVE event in Las Vegas (this isn't exactly digital because we have 1,000+ students show up in Las Vegas to learn – however it is still made possible due to all our students we brought into our online course from all around the world).
- Q&A sessions with our coaches, right from your computer.

This is just the tip of the iceberg!

Profit Academy literally deploys everything about creating an amazing digital product and has it one place.

To learn more about joining the Profit Academy, please attend our

Free Profit Workshop (or watch the replays) at
www.FreeProfitWorkshop.com. The free training will help you
decide whether Profit Academy is really for you and whether you
qualify to be a student!

Creating Digital Products Is So Easy Now!

I understand that the concept of creating your own digital
product might sound intimidating, but take my word for it: It's very
simple. I'm dedicating an entire section in the Free Profit Workshop
simply to teaching you just how to create your own product (most of
it using very inexpensive outsourcing). Please make sure to register
to attend the Free LIVE Event, all hosted on the Internet. Register
here: www.FreeProfitWorkshop.com. Even if you miss the LIVE
presentation, you can still watch the replay before we take the entire
training series down!

All right, back to creating digital products:

Twenty years ago, creating a product with audio and video
was expensive and time consuming. You needed expensive
equipment if you wanted to create even a semi-professional product.
Video cameras would cost you nearly $3,000 and a good microphone
could be as expensive as $1,000. That was just the beginning. You
also had to hire an expensive editing expert to put it all together.

However, time have really changed *(and fast)*. Digital
products are incredibly easy to create now and can be done on a
shoestring budget. Most common laptops and computers now come
pre-loaded with the necessary software and equipment. Even if you
want to go out and buy equipment, you can be ready to prepare
professional content for less than $100 in equipment cost!

At this point, though, you do not even need to invest $100.
You can create much of the content for absolutely free.

How I Created $1 Million From My Wife's Closet

It's crazy to see how far we have come in technology in the last ten years alone. When I started, if I wanted to get an audio recording done. I had two choices. I could either spend upwards to $5,000 buying the needed equipment or I could spend even more hiring an audio studio.

It was so hard and expensive to do!

Today, you can take even the least expensive laptop and it has professional grade audio software already built in! You can then get a microphone for around $100 that will rival any professional studio!

Over a year ago, I had an idea for a great product I wanted to create in the personal development niche. I wanted it to be all audio. In comes my wife's closet.

I was roaming the house doing sound tests and had an echo problem everywhere. The sound wasn't coming as nicely as I wanted. That is until I had an idea...

What about my wife's closet!

See, her closet is full of clothes. There is no better way to dampen an echo than to surround yourself with clothes! I dragged a chair into the closet. There was a ironing board in there already. I set my laptop on the ironing board and held my microphone right in my hand.

In less than five hours (all shot in just one day), I had just created an amazing dream product that would impact the lives of thousands of people!

I went on to create over $1 million in sales with that product in less than a year. My total budget to create it had been just the microphone (which is mine forever to record as many products as my heart desires).

Who would have ever thought? The more clothes my wife buys, the more money I can make!

    The real key is to have valuable content. The technical tools need to produce that content is now the easy part. You can have all that done in just one day if you want. However, we need to take time and make sure that you have an excellent product that creates hordes of raving fans all over the world.

    Let's keep pushing along. I want to show you just how to create digital products worth $1 million. I also want to show you some secrets that can help you seriously multiply the profits you make from every customer you ever get.

Chapter 14
Creating a Digital Product Worth $1 Million

I'm going to take you through a crash course now on how to simply and quickly create your first profitable digital product. If you want more hands-on help, then you have two options:

1. Attend the Free Profit Workshop

Please go to: www.FreeProfitWorkshop.com and you can attend our LIVE training sessions or you can also watch the replays of the workshop (depending on when you visit the site).

There are three free training sessions in the entire workshop and I get into far more detail and actually use whiteboards, PowerPoint, and LIVE interviews with experts to share with you in a lot more detail.

2. Enroll into the Profit Academy

We have very limited seats for the Profit Academy program and you have to qualify to enroll; however, our students are among the most successful digital publishers on the Internet. If you are interested in learning more, just attend our Free Profit Workshop (or watch the replays)!

Now, let's get into the steps for creating your first *digital product.*

The process is broken into five main steps

Step #1 – Finalizing Your Niche: Is It a $1 Million Niche?
Step #2 – Finding a Great Domain Name
Step #3 – Discovering Your Hook: Naming Your Product
Step #4 – Creating Your Outline
Step #5 – Creating Your Product

I want to start by asking you not to skip any of the steps. I also do not want you to change any of the steps. The process I am showing you is time-tested for over a decade and over thousands of students.

It works. Period.

The process is also very simple and easy to implement. Any changes to the process will only make it more difficult and create more roadblocks for you to go through. Keep it simple. Keep it easy. Take action and move fast!

Chapter 15
Step #1 – Finalizing Your Niche: Is It a $1 Million Niche?

When I first started trying to make money online about 13 years ago, I made a crucial mistake that cost me seven months and the little money I had. The mistake was in choosing the wrong niche (*passion*) to launch my business in. I jumped the gun without doing my research and made the assumption that my idea would be incredibly profitable.

That was the first and last time I ever made that mistake.

Today, I believe in firmly researching any idea I have. I don't believe in taking big risks, only calculated ones. In this step, you are going to learn two simple metrics that you absolutely must check before ever considering launching into a specific passion.

Although most all passions can be turned into $1 million, there most certainly are certain passions that cannot be. Within just two steps and less than a few hours, you will be able to determine just which of your passions will be the most profitable.

How to test your passion:

- Are there enough people who share your passion?
- Are these people willing to spend money on this passion?

These are the only two things you need to undoubtedly determine. Again, with the power of the Internet, it is fortunately very easy to do so.

Research Metric #1: Is There a Market?

In just minutes you can know whether there are enough people around the world who share your passion. You have a choice of two different great tools in determining the market size:

- Google Adwords: Keyword Planner
- SEMRush.com (provides 10 free searches)

The definition of *keyword research* is when you get a chance to take a peek behind the search engines in the world (especially

Google). The search tools provide you a great resource to be able type in a keyword and then see how many people around the world (or even by country) have searched for that keyword recently.

The Keyword Planner tool by Google is by far the most popular; however, there is only one catch with using the tool provided by Google. You need to activate your advertising account with them first. You will have to go in and create a fictitious ad in order to get access. Google will require you to act as if you are preparing an ad and input your credit card details as well. However, at the very last moment, you can turn the ad off and never spend a dime (but gain full access to their Free keyword research tool).

The process of having to pretend to launch an ad and also enter a credit card number makes some students feel uncomfortable. Keyword research at the level we need to do it (just for niche evaluation) does not require such an advanced tool as Google's Keyword Planner.

For that reason, we recommend our students use www.SEMRush.com. This tool is free, instant to use, and provides just enough information to help you determine the size of your niche.

The following screenshots have been taken at the time of writing this book. The user interface may be slightly different by the time you are using the service; however, the overall service should remain the same.

Go to SEMRush.com

* * *

The first step is to figure out a good keyword that represents your niche. For example, if you want to build a business around the world of personal development, perhaps your topic of choice is *law of attraction.*

In that case, you want to type in "law of attraction" into the keyword search area.

Let's say you are very passionate about weight loss and fitness. You could start your search by typing in "weight loss" into this keyword area.

Your keyword should be targeted but also general. For example, "law of attraction" is a perfect keyword to analyze the niche, however "how to apply the law of attraction" would be too specific for this purpose.

The next page you get will look something like this:

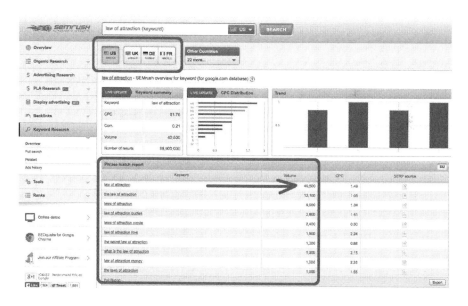

A few things to note here:

1. Data from only the United States is selected.

This is absolutely fine for the purpose of our search. We are simply trying to see the demand of one idea (*niche*) versus another one. In that scenario, we do not need to dig any deeper.

2. The search volume being shown is the average monthly searched for that keyword over a 12-month period. In this case it is showing that the keyword was searched for an average of 40,500 times per month.

Always remember one thing, we are doing a quick "lay of the land" search here. This does not mean that your market only has 40,500 people in it. There are literally hundreds of keywords that target your passion. If we were to total them all up, you would most likely come into the hundreds of thousands (if not millions).

Again, our purpose now is to simply compare your different passions and put them up against each other to see which will be the most likely candidate for profit. In that scenario, we only need to use one keyword.

Let's compare this now to another idea to show you the drastic difference. Let's assume you have a passion for rock skipping (I'm using an absurd example on purpose.) Here is what you would see:

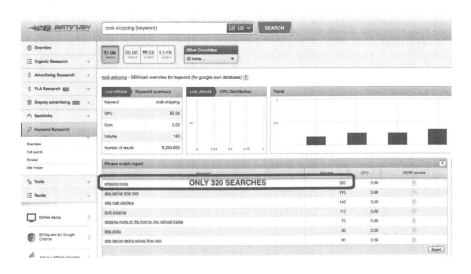

You can quickly see the vast difference. *Law of attraction* had 40,500 searches and *rock skipping* has only 320 searches. Immediately you can start see what it takes to see a sizable market.

After spending months playing with this tool, I have come to determine the following rough estimates. Remember, nothing is written in stone; these numbers can be changed and depending on the niche, they might not be accurate. What I did was simply type in niches that I know to be excellent and compare the search volumes with niches that I know to be bad.

After doing this for long enough, I came up with the following averages:

0 – 3,000 Searches	Absolutely Not a Profitable Niche
3,000 – 5,000 Searches	Slightly Profitable Niche
5,000 – 15,000 Searches	$1 Million Niche (*Sweet Spot*)
15,000 – 40,000 Searches	Very Profitable (*but competitive*)
40,000+ Searches	Incredibly Profitable (*very competitive*)

This is just the beginning. The first major step here is to make sure that your passion has at least 5,000 minimum searches on this tool (per month). As far as competition is concerned, I have never worried too much about it. There will always be opportunities in the most competitive niches as well, if you use our system.

One key thing to remember: Just because a niche has 100,000 or more searches does not necessarily make it a great passion for you to launch a business in. Our next research step is going to help protect you from making this mistake. Let me show you an example. If you search for the word "recipes," you will see that it is searched over 450,000 times a month on Google alone. However, ask anyone who has tried to build a digital empire selling recipes and they will tell you just how difficult it is!

The next step we are going to do will make sure that you guarantee your niche will be easy to profit in as well.

Research Metric #2: Does Your Market Spend Money?

The first niche I ever created a product in, I never took the time to do this step. I launched a product in the "how to study in college" space purely based on the fact that there are millions of students in college. Surely, they want to learn how to get better grades.

I then found that no one else, on the entire Internet, was selling a product like this. I was dumbfounded and so excited that I had chills running down my back. I firmly believed that I had cracked the code. I thought I was going to be a millionaire before the year was over!

I guess I was naïve back then.

I found myself to be so brilliant that no one else on the entire Internet had thought of my niche. I was going to be the only one in the world selling this information and would therefore, immediately be successful.

I spent seven months of my life building this product and spending whatever little money I had. When time came to start selling it, I couldn't be more excited. That is until the first 24 hours went by and I did not have a single sale. Then, the first week went by and I still did not have a single sale. Sadly enough, even 30 days went by without my generating a single sale.

That was a very valuable lesson for me. I walked away learning something about the word *competition*.

Competition is good. No competition is very bad.

The basic theory here is that if others are successfully doing something, it becomes that much easier for you to do it, too. We want to build a $1 million business; we don't want to take unnecessary risks!

I believe in following existing models. I avoid re-inventing the wheel, whenever I can. Just the fact that no one else was successfully selling in the "how to study in college" should have been clue enough for me to stay out of the topic all together.

After that mistake, I have always made sure that I find a good number of competitors in any topic before I ever consider building a business in it. Fortunately, thanks to the Internet again, I can fully research a niche in just minutes and know whether it's a niche where people spend money or not.

1. Go to Clickbank.com

Clickbank.com is a digital product marketplace. They have been around for over a decade and continue to be one of the leading companies that aggregate digital products in one marketplace. Clickbank does all the payment processing for the person who owns the product, and they also do all the affiliate tracking.

It is said that they have more than 10,000 digital products you can choose from (as an affiliate). You can have all your affiliate commissions accumulated in one place and paid out on time, every time!

Besides the fact that Clickbank.com is an excellent place to process your payments and find great products to promote as an affiliate, Clickbank.com is also an excellent source for market research.

Considering that they have 10,000+ products on there, it is safe to say that Clickbank.com has covered almost about any profitable niche in the market! I have mostly found that if it is not successfully selling on Clickbank.com, it is not going to successfully sell on the Internet, period.

Here is how you access the Clickbank marketplace: https://accounts.clickbank.com/marketplace.htm

On the left side, you will see a list of categories, you can start searching there. Whenever you click a category, Clickbank will show you a list of the top selling products in that category. Let's do an example:

* * *

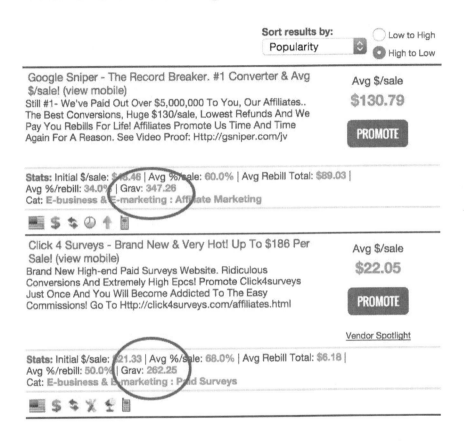

I went into the E-business and E-marketing category and immediately see a product called "Google Sniper." Besides all the other great data that Clickbank is showing me, for the purposes of niche research, my interest is solely in the gravity score (as circled in the picture above).

You can see that the top two products in this niche have gravity scores of 347.26 and 2562.25. If I continue down the list, I see that even product #10 on the first page has a gravity of 65.21.

What does the Clickbank gravity stand for?

The truth is that no one really knows the exact answer. Clickbank does not tell you; they say it's a proprietary formula. However, one thing that no one argues is that the higher this number, the better.

More specifically, I try to find niches where at least five to six of the top products all have high gravities. The E-business space happens to have very high gravities, but even products that have gravities of 30 or so have been proven to do well on Clickbank.

Again, the key is not to just find one or two products; you want to find quite a few in that category, all of them doing well. Let's go back to the recipe example we were using before. The word "recipe" had more than 450,000 searches a month, but I warned that it might not be a good niche.

Well, let's see if Clickbank.com proves me right or wrong.

* * *

Cooking, Food & Wine : Recipes

Now, this is interesting.

Clickbank has proven me right AND wrong at the same time. As you can see if you keep scrolling down, the gravity by the time I reach #10 is only .88. What this tells me is that the top products in this category are the only ones selling. They could be selling well for any various reasons; perhaps the product is by a celebrity or someone with a big brand.

However, this research also showed me something else very interesting. Out of the top four products selling well in the cooking niche, three of them are about the paleo diet. Now, if that is not powerful research, I don't know what is!

There is one more resource that can really easily tell you whether your market is willing to spend money in your niche or not. It is a very simple website and it takes only a few minutes to explore your niche.

2. Go to Magazines.com

In my years online I have found that if a particular topic has enough people with a burning passion who are willing to spend, there will almost always be a magazine on the topic.
- Watches
- Sports
- Weight Loss
- Fitness
- Business
- Entrepreneurship
- Finance and Investing

Just go to Magazines.com and see if your passion has a magazine dedicated to it. If it does, you are most likely in good shape. However, I still recommend tying that research together with a quick review of Clickbank.com

There you have it!

As you can see, you can do all the steps above in less than an hour. It might be the best hour you ever spend in your business assuring that you don't waste any of your time or money going into a niche that doesn't stand a chance.

Now that you have found the perfect passion for building your business, let's move to the next step.

Chapter 16
Step #2 – Finding a Great Domain Name

Finding a domain name is a key step. In many cases, students move on to the next steps and start working on those while spending a bit of time every day researching domain names.

According to the last published number by TechCrunch, there are over 250 million domain names registered around the world of which 50% are *.com*. Obviously, this means that finding a domain name can be tricky! However, I always insist that my students don't give up easily.

Head on over to either GoDaddy.com or NameCheap.com and start typing in domain name ideas and search until you find a great domain name that fits at least most of the criteria that I give below.

Another great tool to help you is DomainsBot.com. This is a tool that allows you to type in a keyword and it will automatically show you domain name ideas that are currently available.

What To Look For In a Good Domain Name

Here are some rules I like to follow:
- Always a *.com* (*since we're building a brand, I prefer .com*)
- Short, catchy, and memorable (*no more than three words*)
- Easy to type and spell (*yoursubconscious.com is not a good example; many will misspell that domain name.*)
- Use power words. The domain name itself should send a message.

Look at ProfitAcademy.com as an example. It is very clear what we are doing here. Just from the domain name, you can tell that I have created an academy (elite training and community) for individuals looking to make a profit.

Straightforward. Simple. Easy to remember and powerful.

This is what you are looking for when it comes to a good domain name.

This is a step that you can do concurrently as you move on to the next steps. If it takes you some time to figure it out, don't worry. Some of our best students have taken days before they found a domain name they loved.

Should You Buy an Existing Domain Name?

Many times you will come upon a domain name that you are researching and it is up for sale. The decision to buy or not to buy is really your own. If you absolutely love the domain name and can easily afford to pay for it, then go for it!

There have been many domain names that I have chosen to buy. However, I never did this in the beginning. When you're just starting, I prefer you buy an imperfect domain name and use your funds instead to invest in traffic. However, the choice is completely yours.

I will say this if it helps. Getting a super domain name versus getting a good domain name will make almost no difference to the results you get (profit) which is in the end all we really care about at the moment.

Keep it simple and save your money. Find a domain that is still available. The easiest way to do this is to pick three power words and combine them. Keep searching; there has never been a situation in which either I or any of my students have not eventually found a domain name that we love and that will do great justice to our online business.

Now that you have your domain name, let's keep moving forward and determine what your unique hook is and what you should name your product!

Chapter 17
Step #3 – Discovering Your Hook: Naming Your Product

Before we can begin to outline and create your product, I like to name the product. The process of determining the hook actually helps create the outline. (Often, just the hook discovery can be 90% of the battle.)

The best way to learn good hooks is too look at a few examples:

- How to Lose 10 Pounds in 10 days.
- The 1 Wall Street Secret That Made This Guy $5 Million
- How to Make $10,000 in 30 Days or Less
- 3 Steps to Ranking on Page of Google in 7 Days or Less
- 7 Ways To Find the Job of Your Dreams
- Master Microsoft Excel in Just 5 Hours

As you can see, all these hooks have one thing in common. They all deliver a definite promise and many times, even in a defined period. The purpose of a hook is to grab your reader's attention almost instantly. A great hook is almost a promise in and of itself.

The key to a hook is to use a powerful statement that delivers a vision or a promise that many in your niche would find enticing. I prefer using shorter hooks. I always try to get mine to just one sentence. Sometimes this can be difficult, but if you massage your message for a little bit of time, I find that most can get it down to that single sentence!

I find that one of the easiest ways to do this exercise is to see what your top competitors are doing. What are their hooks? If they are successfully selling their product, it's safe to assume that their hook is working.

Go to Clickbank.com and make a list of the top five products in your category. From there, write down that product's hook. You will start to see a trend. Use that as a good base to start from and then angle your own hook right in there!

* * *

Naming Your Product

The name of your product is an exercise that merges your domain name with your hook. Sometimes, it can be as simple as combining the both of them!

Let's use the Profit Academy as an example. The name of this product is really *Profit Academy: How to Turn Your Passion Into $1 Million.* The first part (on the left side of the colon) happens to be my domain name and the second part (on the right side of the colon) is my hook. It worked out perfectly for me!

I find many times that if you are using a three-word domain name (as discussed in Step #2), you can easily make that domain name into your product.

Remember, you are just starting. Nothing has to be perfect yet. The key is to execute! Do not get stuck on this step. The beauty of a digital business is that you can change anything at any time. The name of the product can even change in the future if you really want it to.

For now, pick something powerful that makes a statement and that you like and run with it!

Now that you have your niche, your domain name and your hook, it's time to dig your heels into the main product. Let's start by creating the outline of your product.

Chapter 18
Step #4 – Creating Your Product Outline

Creating your product outline is genuinely most of the battle. Once you have the details of what will be in your product, the rest is very easy to do. You can even outsource most of it! For the purposes of this book, we are going to go over just one of the ways of creating your outline.

Please keep in mind that the strategies can change slightly based on the kind of product you are creating, the length of it, and of course, the topic. However, the following is what most of my Profit Academy students have used to outline their first product in a matter of just 60 minutes or less!

When creating your outline, I ask that you follow this formula:

Task #1 – Name Your Modules (*the same as chapters*)
Task #2 – Name Your Sections (*the same as sub-chapters*)
Task #3 – Create Bullet Points for Each Section
Task #4 – Assign Media Formats to Each Section

I have watched countless students complete this entire process within 60 minutes or less right before my eyes. I will give you one key resource to use when creating your outline, and very few information marketers ever use it *(*yet it's right in front of us and only a mouse click away)!

Amazon.com

Go to Amazon.com and search for a book that is related to your topic of choice. For the following example, I searched for "investing in stocks." The first book that came up for me, I clicked on the title of the book.

As soon as I click on the title, I want to you to look to the top right corner of the image of the book:

* * *

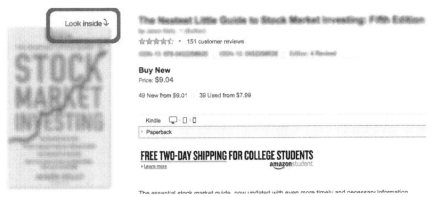

(I've blurred out the title and the cover of the book out of respect to the author.)

As soon as you click on the "Look Inside" image, a new window will open. This window will allow you to read the first few pages of the book. Almost every book on Amazon allows you to at least see the table of contents of the book.

I think you can see where I'm going with this, right?

Now, please note that I will never ever condone plagiarizing or copying someone else's hard work. That is not right and not legal. However, if you were to look into the top 10 books in your niche and simply review their table of contents to determine what topics are the most popular in your niche, there is nothing wrong with that!

I do this all the time.

I will scan the table of contents of many different books and that always sparks idea for my own outline. Now that you have this ultimate resource in your hands, let's dive into the details of each task.

Task #1 – Name Your Modules (or Chapters)

I have found that if you are creating a *course*, you should call the chapters *modules*. It carries a higher perceived value. Most people are used to relating chapters with books. Books are sold for less than $10. Hence, creating that link in someone's mind will devalue your course and make the buyer feel that it is simply a book.

Assuming I am creating one product, I will break that product into five to ten modules. This means that I will break my course into five to ten main chapters or topics that need to covered. That is all task #1 is.

For example, if you are building a product on weight loss, your Task #1 might look something like:

Module 1: Introduction and My Story
Module 2: Determining Your Perfect Weight
Module 3: The Perfect and Easy Diet
Module 4: The 30-Minute Fitness Program
Module 5: Your Personal 30-Day Plan
Module 6: Delicious Recipes That Shed Pounds
Module 7: Conclusion and Action Steps

This would be an example of a great product in the making. I literally finished task #1 as I was writing this in three minutes flat.

Task #1 is as simple as that, but please do take some time to research competing products and make sure your product is covering the necessary information. Once we have Task #1 completed, we move on to the next one.

Task #2 – Name Your Sections

Each module should be broken down into three to five sections. Doing this again adds more perceived value to your course and also helps you keep the course organized. Each topic of course can be easily broken down (considering that the main module titles are still almost always very general).

This is again a process in which using Amazon.com can be very helpful.

Let's carry forward with the same example and build it out:

* * *

Module 1: Introduction and My Story
What Is This Book About?
Why Am I Writing This Book?
What Will You Learn in This Book
My Personal Story

Module 2: Determining Your Perfect Weight
Are You Actually Overweight or Just Out of Shape?
The Three Weight Indexes : Which Is the Best One?
The Exact Formula to Use

Module 3: The Perfect and Easy Diet
Do Calories Matter?
What Foods Should You Avoid?
What Foods Should You Eat?
Sample Meal Plans For the Day
Important Weight Loss Nutrition Your Body Needs
Dietary Supplements to Help You Lose Weight

Module 4: The 30-Minute Fitness Program
Key Exercises That You Must Do
How Much and How Often Should You Exercise
Sample Workout Plan to Follow

Module 5: Your Personal 30-Day Plan
How to Create a Personalized Plan
Your Plan Formula
Sample Plan and How To Execute

Module 6: Delicious Recipes That Shed Pounds
Breakfast Recipes
Lunch Recipes
Dinner Recipes
Snack Recipes

Dessert Recipes

Module 7: Conclusion and Action Steps
Summary of Modules
Common Obstacles to Watch For
Motivational Story
Final Words and Action Steps

There you have it. You don't even know it yet, but your outline is nearly done. Even if I stopped now and handed this to a good writer, he or she could take it from here and completely finish my course for me.

However, the more you give your writer, the higher quality your course will be.

Now, it's time to move on.

Task #3 – Create Bullet Points For Each Sub-Chapter

It really depends on who is creating this product and his or her aptitude on the topic. This task can be skipped sometimes. However, it does not take more than 30 minutes to finish this task as well so I recommend my students finish it anyway.

Task #2 was to take the main modules and break them down to three to five sub-topics. Well, you are going to do the same exercise one more time, this time with the sections. Each section can still be broken down into more bullet points you want to use. For the sake of saving time, I will do just one of the modules from the above example for you.

Module 2: Determining Your Perfect Weight

Are You Actually Overweight or Just Out of Shape?
- The definition of being overweight
- The difference between overweight and out of shape
- The weight scale: Are you overweight?
- What part of your weight is just water weight?

The Three Weight Indexes: Which Is The Best One?
- Index #1
- Index #2
- Index #3
- The benefits and negatives of each one, and which should you
follow?

The Exact Formula to Use
- Final calculation of your weight
- Determining just how overweight you are

Again, this step can also be very easily done if you have access to about five to ten top books on the same topic. These books will help you brainstorm and make sure that you are not leaving any key topic undiscussed.

Task #4 – Assign Media Formats To Each Section

This task is something I started to do for myself as it helped me organize my thoughts and my project management during course creation. If you intend to do a product that is all written, this task can be skipped. However, if you plan on adding audio and video, this next step takes only two minutes but can be very helpful when you're actually creating the product.

As always, nothing is better than an example. I will take two sections from the previous outline and use them as examples:

Module 1: Introduction and My Story
What Is This Book About? *(Written)*
Why Am I Writing This Book? *(Video)*
What Will You Learn in This Book *(Video)*
My Personal Story *(Video)*

Module 2: Determining Your Perfect Weight
Are You Actually Overweight or Just Out of Shape? *(Written)*
The Three Weight Indexes: Which Is The Best One? *(Written)*
The Exact Formula to Use *(Written)*

Notice how I just added a *(Written)* or a *(Video)* next to each topic. This way when I dive in to create the product, I know exactly what to do and how to set up for it.

Well, there you have it. As long as you have Amazon.com, creating your outline should be pretty fast and easy. You might have a product already inside of you and might not even need Amazon.com. Trust me, once you do it one time, you're going to fall in love with this process.

Chapter 19
Step #5 – Creating Your Product

Now that the outline is done, there is only one thing left: create the product. There are two options when it comes to creating your product.

- Write or record it on your own
- Outsource it for a very small budget

In my company, I have a standard rule that seems to have served me very well.

"If the product is written, outsource it. If it's audio, outsource the script. If it's video, I'll make the outline, turn the camera on, and record it myself."

I don't expect everyone to follow the same rule; however, it has worked well for me. The power of outsourcing is incredible lately. With talent from all over the world now at our fingertips using simple freelance websites (for a ridiculously small budget), it almost feels like a crime to not use outsourcing.

As you can tell, I've gone into a rant about outsourcing because I absolutely feel that everyone should use it. During the Free Profit Workshop, especially on Workshop #2 (February 26th at 8:00 p.m. Eastern), I am going to spend a good amount of time outlining just how to do outsourcing. Also, in a few moments I will get further into detail in this book as well.

But, first—what if you want to create the product yourself?

Creating The Product Yourself

There are three main types of products you can create yourself. I will give you a crash course on each one. To really get into more details, you will need to watch the Free Profit Workshop trainings or even better, enroll into the Profit Academy program.

Also remember, there is no one right way of creating a product. There are literally thousands of approaches and everyone will have a unique approach. What I am going to do is share with you some techniques that have worked the best for me and my Profit Academy students.

I am also going to make a special effort to share specific strategies that allow you to create the entire course on a tiny budget, an almost laughable budget!

Creating a Written Product

If you are going to write your own product, you don't need much equipment. Any computer with a program like Pages or Microsoft Word will be sufficient. After you finish writing, you simply export it as a PDF and you're done!

One step that will really help you write the product is to take the outline and go one level deeper on the bullet points. This way you would have:
- Module Title
  - o Section Title
    - Bullet Point
      - Sub-Bullet Point

The deeper you keep going and the more bullet points you add, you will notice that the course practically begins to write itself!

Creating an Audio Product

When I create an audio product, I treat it the same as a written product, only I write the product in a more conversational tone so that I can later read it out loud. However, I would still recommend the same thing: Create a deeper level outline with more bullet points.

The only other piece of equipment you will now need is a good microphone. If this is your first product and you are just starting, you will be served just fine with a good headset microphone. Many can be found for less than $20 at your local electronics store. Even if you want to go professional, I recommend investing in the *Blue Yeti* microphone that costs just over $100 (and is well worth the investment).

My favorite part about these microphones is that the technology has gotten so good that you no longer require a professional audio studio. To buffer sound and avoid echo, I personally simply record in my wife's closet. You heard me right—her closet! She has a walk-in closet and it is full of clothes. The clothes help block any echoes out.

I take my laptop inside, I set it on a chair and hold the microphone as I read my scripted product. That's it; nice and simple. Most computers now have software that will record your audio. I use Macs and they come with *Garageband*, a perfect application for recording a product!

Creating a Video Product

There are three kinds of video products you can create.
*   Face to Camera
*   Screen Capture
*   Webinars and Replays

Face to camera videos are when you set a video camera down and record yourself speaking to the camera. My tenure of working with thousands of students has taught me that many students are comfortable in front of a video camera. If you are not comfortable in front of a camera, there is no need to put yourself through that. There are easier options.

Also when you do face to camera, you need to pay special attention to the quality of video and sound. You need to have good lighting and the proper settings on the camera, ideally. If the quality of the shoot is poor, the product could work against you.

Personally, I use a professional video team every time I ever shoot a face to camera video for a product. I find that it is easier; however, such a team definitely requires a good budget.

Screen capture is a video that is made when software on your computer simply records your screen and your voice. Your face never shows up on the camera. You can prepare PowerPoint slides ahead of time and simply do a voiceover. I have found that students love these videos and there is virtually no editing needed nor any concern about quality.

The same microphone you plan on using for the audio product can be used here. For screen capture, I am a big fan of two software programs (depending on whether you are using PC or MAC):

- PC = Camtasia ($299)
- MAC = ScreenFlow ($99)

I have gotten more value out of my ScreenFlow purchase than I can ever explain. This software might be one of the best investments I have ever made.

Webinars and replays are very similar to screen-capture videos. The main difference is that you are conducting them LIVE and then having them recorded as well. This would theoretically allow you to start selling the product without even having made the product. You can sell customers a product that is delivered over a certain number of weeks.

This way you can start getting sales and start creating your product as you go. Again, products like this are usually going to be based around PowerPoint. You would use the same microphone we have already discussed and run it all on your computer. If you use a platform like *GoToWebinar* to run your webinar, the software will even automatically record the entire webinar presentation for you.

As you can see, creating your own product is actually very easy once your main outline is done. The outline is most of the battle and I have already shared the best resource in the world to help you quickly create the best outline possible: Amazon.com

Now, what if you don't want to create your own product? What if you want to outsource it (this is how I built my initial empire)? I am a big believer in the power of outsourcing, especially when you are just beginning. Outsourcing can drastically reduce your risk and your time to market and can create a higher quality product!

Using Outsourcing to Create Your Product

In my business, in the last 13 years, it would be impossible for me to even calculate just how many times I have used outsourcing. Even today, I use outsourcing on a daily basis. With simple freelance websites now giving us access to talent around the entire world (especially at such steep international discounts), it's almost crazy not to use outside help.

I like using outsourcing for a few reasons:
- I get more done, and quicker.
- I get to scale into more projects at the same time.
- I can focus on marketing and list building.
- Content is well researched and better written.
- I can work on more than one product at a time. (This helps me build my funnel a lot faster; something we discuss in the next part of this book.)
- It saves me a ton of money.
- Finding long-term talent to work with for years.
- Many, many more reasons.

My very first team member I ever brought into the company was first found as a outsourcing relationship. The first time I ever had a technical project, I used outsourcing. The first time I ever needed a website put up, I used outsourcing. I don't use outsourcing just for content creation; I use it to run many parts of my business. However, I have found it the most useful in the area of content creation.

There are a few steps involved in doing very well with outsourcing:
1. Choose a freelance website.
2. Post your project.
3. Choose a freelancer.
4. Manage the work output.
5. Build a strong relationship for recurring work.

The best situation is when you have spent a few months building up consistent relationships that you use over and over in your business. Suddenly you never have to post jobs and review the applications; you can simply fire off an email or a Skype message and a few days later, the work is done!

#1 – Choose a Freelance Website
There are quite a few great ones that you can use. I use different ones, depending on the kind of work I have. Here are a few key ones that are popular:

- o Freelancer.com
- o Guru.com
- o eLance.com
- o 99Designs.com

Freelancer.com is a great resource if you are looking for offshore developers. They offer all services, but I have found them best for simple and small project-based technical development.

Guru.com has been a gold mine for me to find talent that is Western-based with excellent English language and grammar skills to help me create my products. The pricing for Guru vendors is more than other sites, but that is also because they cater a lot to talent from Western countries.

eLance.com is an excellent source for all-around help. eLance also provides a lot of Western-based talent for almost any kind of work. I have not personally used this site very much, but that is only because I have found great resources at Guru.com and just built my loyalty there.

99Designs.com is an excellent resource for design projects; however, it is much more costly than any other freelance website. The greatest benefit of using 99Designs is that instead of hiring a designer blindly and hoping she or he does a good job, you can actually get a group of them to do the job first and then reward one of them the project money. That way you know exactly what you are buying before paying for it.

If you are just beginning, 99Designs.com may be too advanced (and too costly) for your focus right now.

"Have you ever heard the phrase "Jack of all trades but master of none"? As a company, we have quite a few ninjas on the team who are jacks of all trades, but there are certain areas of our business where we really need those REAL MASTERS. We turn to outsourcing to seek out masters in certain fields to get tasks and projects done quickly and efficiently. Outsourcing allows our company to work faster AND save money."

* * *

Meredith Marlin
Vice President – Operations
VSS Media, Inc.

#2 – *Post Your Project*

I have one major rule with posting a job on any of these sites. I take the most time I can to get as detailed as possible with my posting. I also put enough in there that allows me to immediately tell if the freelancer has even ready my post. (Many freelancers will send you a private message after they bid on your work).

I despise it when I get their cut-and-pasted private messages that are clearly sent to everyone, no matter what work is being bid on. This way when I put details in the project post, I can tell if they are really sending me a private message based on my job description.

Hold nothing back. Take an extra day if you have to before putting up the post, but make it as complete as possible.

#3 – *Choose a Freelancer*

In my years of experience of working with Freelancers, I have developed some standard rules I follow when selecting someone.

- Never choose the least expensive nor the most expensive bid. Choose somewhere in between.
- The person must have a minimum rating of 9.5 and at least 10 projects completed on the website. (I do not work with new people on the platform).
- Always send a private message and see how fast the freelancer will respond to you. (I prefer those who can respond in 12 hours or less).
- Have at least a few private messages back and forth to get a good feeling for the person before picking anyone.
- Read the person's reviews. Instead of only looking at star ratings, actually go in and read what past employers are writing about them. I like to pick freelancers whose past employers have left raving

reviews.

It really is not more complicated than that. If you follow these simple rules, you are likely to find someone great!

#4 – Manage the work output

I don't believe in micro-management; however, I also have trust issues. When I bring on a new freelancer, I make sure to stay in touch on a daily basis until the project is complete. I likely do it again for the next two to three projects as well. If the freelancer can complete at least three projects for me on time and without any issues, that is when I finally start to reduce the micro-management.

Initially, I use the private messaging system inside the freelance website, but I also mostly use Skype to communicate with the freelancer. In rare cases, if it is a bigger project, I will get on regular phone calls as well.

When the freelancer has first started, I also ask him or her to send me drafts of the work for my intermittent review. When someone new starts working with you, to be fair; she or he doesn't know your style at first. It can definitely take a few days (or even weeks) for someone new to learn your preferences.

It is very important that you make your self available to work with the freelancer initially and offer hands-on guidance, or else your work will never be of quality.

I also make sure I am constantly in touch with the freelancer so there's no chance to slip and forget about my work. Freelancers have a consistent habit of taking on more work than they can handle. When that happens, they will regularly juggle based on which client is the loudest and most up to date. If you are constantly in touch and engaged, they will not have the opportunity to put your work on the back burner.

Although this might sound tedious, it is not that bad. It just requires you to do a check-in once a day. Soon after that freelancer has worked with you a few times, you can slow down on the check-ins!

#5 – Build a Strong Relationship for Recurring Work

There is no better feeling than to never have to search on freelance websites and to be able to go straight to someone and assign work. Especially once this person gets to know you and your style, it will be a blessing. I would say that about 70% of the freelancers I have worked with in my life have been the kinds who have stuck around for quite some time.

One of the benefits of having a qualifying round in the beginning is that you bring in better freelancers from the start. This allows you to have a better pool of candidates in your company for future work.

When a project ends, you should immediately try to keep that freelancer engaged if you can. If you can work with him or her closely for at least a month or more, you will see a special relationship build. Suddenly, you will have priority, better rates, and work being completed faster.

Always look at your freelancing projects as the possibility of finding long-term relationships. This mentality has served me very well.

One Last Word About Product Creation

I feel it's important that I take a minute to mention this next part because I have seen one recurring trend in some students (after having trained thousands). I have seen too many students get stuck in the *perfection trap*. This means the students never get their product done because they are too busy trying to make everything perfect.

The student spends so much time trying to make the product better and better that it is never launched! You should just ask yourself one question: "Is there value in this product?" If your answer is yes, then you are ready to move on to the next step. Remember, one of the brilliant things about having an online business is that you can easily make any changes you want at any time.

Focus on value and focus on execution. That's it.

Do not let yourself get lost in the perfection trap, and put your foot down on making changes after a certain amount of time. Even if it's imperfect, it's something. Your goal needs to be to get the product out there as fast as you can so you can start testing your sales message and all the other factors involved.

Remember, your main passion product is just the beginning.

If you truly want to reach $1 million, you're going to need to have more than one product. You're going to need to build a funnel of products. You're going to need to move on to the next part of the Circle of Profit where we talk about how you can multiply your profits.

This means that there will be other products in the funnel that will need your time as well. Don't just invest all your time in this one product and end up losing bigger on the rest of it.

Once you have your passion product done, the real key to making $1 Million lies in being able increase the value of each customer. In over a decade of testing and executing, I have found a very simple formula that I use to get a minimum 500% increase in my profits (*without ever needing any extra traffic*).

The magic is in building your $1 million funnel. If you're ready to continue, that's what we're going to dive into in the next section!

Section 4

Your $1 Million Sales Funnel

Chapter 20
How To Create Your $1 Million Sales Funnel

Vision is the art of seeing what is invisible to others. —
Jonathan Swift

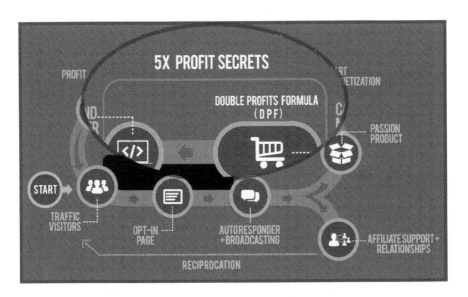

What you're about to learn in this chapter instantly added 500% to my business. I did not get a single extra visitor to my website. I didn't spend a dime extra on the business. All I did was implement a very simple formula and I was able to immediately increase my customer value by 500%!

Customer Value: *The amount of profit generated from a customer through the life-time of that customer.*

So many businesses are so focused on their main passion product that they forget about everything else. Most online marketers become obsessed with getting more traffic to their website. The other marketers spend their time trying to increase their conversions. But so many completely forget the easiest they can do: ***build a proper funnel***.

A Brilliant Backend

There are two terminologies you should get pretty used to:

1. **Frontend**
2. **Backend**

A **frontend** represents all the work that goes on to get visitors to your website and convert those visitors into a sale. Frontend basically represents your main passion product. The process of trying to sell your main passion product is known as the frontend.

A **backend** represents all the products that you can sell to your newly found customer. This means that as soon as someone buys your frontend product, they are now a customer. Well, the relationship has just begun. Your true profits actually lie in your brilliant backend!

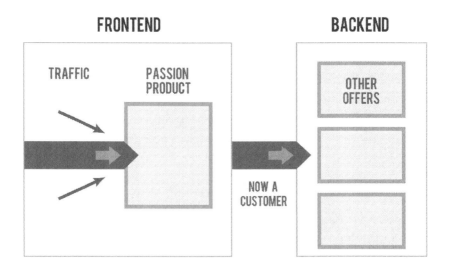

This entire section is about just that: your brilliant backend. I'm going to show you the easiest way to build amazing offers you can turn around very fast and profit from even faster!

* * *

What Is a Sales Funnel?

A **funnel** is a sequence (and in the right order) of products that you offer to your new customer as soon as he or she becomes a customer. Typically (but not always), the price of the products get higher and the level of training and education you offer becomes more advanced and hands-on.

The following is just an example. There are unlimited combinations and kinds of funnels you can create!

You might not realize it, but you have been participating in sales funnels (as a customer) your entire life. Let me give you some examples.

You go to McDonald's and ask for a Big Mac. The cashier immediately responds with, "Would you like fries with that?" You reply, "Yes." The next question the cashier asks you is, "Would you like to add a large Coke?" Again, he makes you think and you decide, "Sure, why not?"

McDonald's just doubled that sale. At first, they were going to earn $3 from that sale; then they generated $6.

Think about the last time you bought a computer at an electronics store. Let's assume the computer cost you $1,000. The store probably makes about a 7% profit on the sale ($70). You're just about to checkout and the sales agent behind the counter offers you a very appealing warranty. "Sir, you should protect your $1,000 investment for three years with our in-store warranty; it only costs $97." Again, you realize that it could be a wise idea.

Most likely the store is partnered with another company, but this time to store probably makes 75% of the sale. That means the store just made another $75 profit on your sale. They just doubled their profit!

Any strong business understands that the best customer is someone who is already a customer. Even better, if you can make additional offers to your customer when she has just agreed to purchase your main product, you will see a tremendous increase in your profits. We consistently see our own business and our students more than double their profits right at the shopping cart!

Just think about it. There is absolutely no risk. You never present a more advanced course or training (at a higher price) until your main passion product has already been sold. These products are only sold to existing customers! This means that there is no chance at ever losing money. You can only make more. Period.

How I Came To Learn About Backend Profits

It happened way back in 2006. I was sitting in a room of marketers. We were all sharing our latest strategies and what we had done. I was very excited. I had amazing numbers to report. In the 12 months before that meeting, I had generated over $1 million and was growing incredibly fast!

I was just one marketer away from sharing my story. I was going to crush it. My story was better than anyone there!

Suddenly, the guy up right before me, starts his part of the discussion with:

"I'm about to hit $3 million and we still have time left this year."

I was shocked. I was even a bit heartbroken. He had just stolen my thunder! I needed to know what he had done. I had spoken to this marketer just months before and he was on track to hitting $1 million, just like me.

The next words out of his mouth changed my business forever.

He said:

"I added an upsell after my frontend product, and it's been huge!"

By the time we met, he didn't just have one upsell. He had built an entire sales funnel. You see, he came from the car business. He, more than anyone else, understood the power of selling your customers more services just as they are buying.

In a car dealership, they try to sell you at least 18 things in addition to the car right when you're signing the contract. Warranties, car servicing, insurance, protection plans, you name it.

He continued to present what a upsell is, what a downsell is and what his "at cart" funnel looks like. I was blown away.

It was time to go back to the drawing board.

Within just 10 days I had implemented everything he taught. We had four months left in the year, at my pace I was expecting to generate about $1.5 million. Just by making a few easy changes, I closed out that year making $3 million.

All because of sales funnels.

Chapter 21
The Secret To Giving Yourself a 500% Raise

Learn to focus on your existing customers and you will see your profits explode. I don't mean to say that you should slow down your traffic or not continue to improve your frontend process. However, if you have to take a two-week break from your frontend to work on your brilliant backend, it will pay off hugely.

I am shocked to see, to this day, how many online business owners are still missing this one piece to the puzzle. Recently, I was helping one of my students, Sammy, who had just launched her first passion product.

Sammy was doing great! She had gone through the entire Profit Academy training in less than six weeks. Within her first two weeks she had been profiting using Phase 1. Now, just six weeks in, she was ready to start Phase 2 by launching her passion product.

Like many, she had ignored the backend completely. She started marketing her passion product using some very simple techniques we teach inside Profit Academy. She was doing very well. Within just six weeks of having started, she was ready to quit her job!

When it came time for me to review her business, the very first thing I noticed is that we needed to add a backend. I sent her a few presentations to watch and told her to immediately implement what they taught. Being a great student, she did just as she was told.

Sammy was able to finish everything in just three weeks.

Three weeks after she had launched her passion product (and already started generating profits), she was ready to now launch her brand new sales funnel.

Here are her numbers:

No Backend	*5X Brilliant Backend*
10,342 Visitors	*10,342 Visitors*
6,089 Subscribers (Phase 1)	*6,089 Subscribers (Phase 1)*
152 Sales at $47	*152 Sales at $47*
$7,144 Sales	*$7,144 Sales*
$3,572 Profit (After Paying Affiliates)	***Brilliant Backend:***
	1. $6,643 Sales ($3,321 Profit) (Using Double Profits Formula)
	2. $11,400 (Using Backend Multiplier)
	Total Profit: $18,293.50
	That's 512% more than what she was doing before!

Without a single extra visitor to her website, Sammy made 512% more money. Think about it, there is a massive difference between $3,572 and $18,293. Imagine how much more investment capital she had the next month to really scale her business!

That's exactly what she did! The next month, she took $10,000 of her $18,293 and reinvested it to get more traffic. Guess what.

She was able to get 21,453 visitors to her website. I'm not kidding. The scale she added was enormous. Her profits shot up and even through today, she is continuing to grow!

All this made possible just because she took three weeks to build a simple backend.

The Two Parts of a Brilliant Backend

There is an unlimited number of things you can do to increase your profits in the backend; however, almost all of them fall into two categories:

1. **Double Profits Formula (DPF)**
2. **Backend Multiplier (BM)**

Your entire business can change even if you just add one of the two above. What I always tell our Profit Academy students is that they should focus on these one at a time.

- First, build your double profits formula backend.
- Second, build your backend multiplier.

If you combine both of the backend strategies, that's when you see 500%+ growth in your profits. Let's take a minute to dive into each of these in greater detail.

Chapter 22
The Double Profits Formula

The Double Profits Formula (DPF) all takes place "at cart." Imagine this: A visitor comes to your website and reads some information (sales material) about your main frontend passion product. He decides to make the wise investment and finish filling out your order page. He clicks *submit* and is now officially your customer.

At this point, you have two options:

1. Send this customer to a thank-you page and give him access to your product.
2. Offer the customer an opportunity to upgrade his order by adding more advanced training (usually at a higher investment).

The DPF always takes place between the frontend purchase and the thank- you page. We also refer to this as "at cart." **At cart** means that the customer is still in your shopping cart. He is still in the buying process and has not actually received access to the course.

Let's use the example of a physical store.

You walk into a store and browse the electronics section. After a few minutes, you find what you are looking for and head to the cash register. From the time you reach that cashier to the time you walk out of the store, you are officially in the DPF territory. Anything we teach for this strategy has to take place in this window.

However, the minute you purchase your item and walk out the door of the store, anything that happens after that is not considered part of the DPF. You would then be in the **backend multiplier** category.

Let's take that same example and move it to the Internet. From the time the customer puts in her credit card information to the time she takes delivery of her purchase, she is still "in the cart" or "at cart."

The Double Profits Formula is what kicks off your sales funnel. It's the first step to building out your 5X Sales Funnel. Let me show you what a typical "at cart" funnel looks like and then what a great DPF sales funnel looks like:

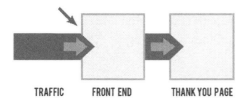

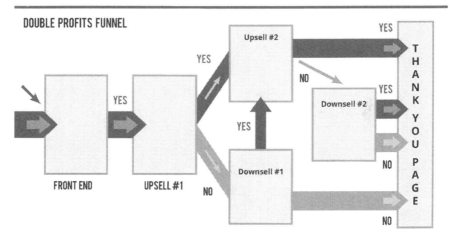

Up through to where the customer is agreeing to purchase your frontend product, nothing changes. However, everything changes the minute she is officially a customer. As you will see, in the "boring" sales funnel, she has reached your thank- you page and is complete.

However, in the double profits funnel, we definitely make it more fun and profitable. Try to keep up as I walk you through this.

#1 – The customer sees "Upsell #1" – This will be the first offer for more advanced training. The customer has a choice to say YES or NO.

#2 – If the customer says YES and purchases this offer, we are in great position to then offer this customer one more upgrade option,

Upsell #2.

However, if the customer says NO and refuses Upsell #1, we will offer what we call a "downsell." (I will explain these terms in details in the next part of this chapter). The downsell is just a less expensive offer or a discount given for the purpose of "saving the sale." Trust me, it works.

#3 – If the customer says NO to the downsell as well, we are going to take her straight to the thank-you page. She has said no twice (back to back) for upgrade options, and it becomes clear that the customer is done.

However, if the customer agrees to buy Downsell #1, we have her back in the "yes loop." We will now take her straight to see Upsell #2.

#4 – On upsell #2, if the customer agrees and says yes, we will now consider the double profits formula to have been a huge success and take her to the thank-you page.

However, if this customer declines upsell #2, we again have the ability to make a "save the sale" offer and take her to downsell #2. Whether or not you use downsell #2 is a personal choice. It does work and it does add sales; however, compared to the rest of the sales funnel, the amount downsell #2 adds is very small.

#5 – If the customer refuses to buy the downsell #2, we again have had two consecutive declines and so we will take the customer straight to the thank-you page.

If the customer agrees to purchase downsell #2, we will still take that customer to the thank-you page. The double profits formula will have been a big success again.

* * *

There you have it!

As you can tell, it can be easy to get carried away with sales funnels. In my 10+ years of experience using sales funnels, I have found it very wise to never offer more than two products directly in the "at cart" funnel.

You are most welcome to offer more products, but you want to do that starting a few days later (which will be what we cover in the backend multiplier section).

How Much Can a Sales Funnel Make You?

All right, I have to do some math now in order to show you the power of a sales funnel. Please try to keep up because we are going to make a ton of assumptions and do some multiplication and division!

Before we start, there are a couple of terms you need to understand.

- **Conversion**. Whenever I say, "This percent converted into a sale," I am referring to the number of people who saw the sales message divided by how many purchased. For example, if I send 1,000 visitors to a sales page and 30 of them choose to buy, I have a conversion rate of 3%. If 300 of them had decided to buy, I would have a conversion rate of 30%.
- **Price**. I think this is self-explanatory. Each of the products has its own price (main product, upsells, and downsells)

All right, let's dive in.

Below is the same funnel, but this time, it contains some assumptions. I have inserted price assumptions and also conversion assumptions. Please note that these numbers are very specific to your situation, and they will change drastically based on your environment, niche, marketing, messaging, and many other factors.

However, the example below is based on more than 10 years of building funnels and having seen hundreds and hundreds of sales funnels that my students have built.

* * *

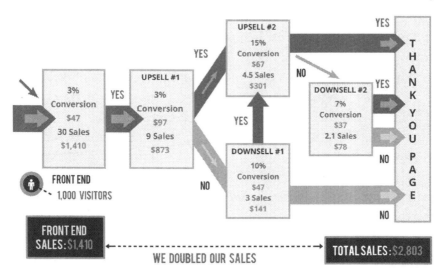

The assumptions above are very conservative. I have actually been able to see far better results as I master the double profits formula. The numbers above are actually what even our beginner-level Profit Academy students are achieving.

There were two kinds of conversion data in this diagram.

- **For the frontend conversion**, it shows only 3% because this will always be your lowest converting product. After all, it is being shown to website visitors who are coming to your website only out of curiosity. You then have to convince them to buy your product.

- **The backend conversions** are showing much larger numbers, as high as 30%. These numbers are much higher because they are being calculated only by your actual customers. Whereas for your frontend conversion, we used 1,000 visitors as our audience number. For the backend conversions, we are only using the number 30. We are only counting the customers.

Always remember that in most cases, your first upsell will always be the higher converting because that is where you have the most attention from your new customer. (After all, she just gave you her credit card!)

As you can see above, we are making a bit of money at each stage of the sales funnel. Perhaps each number on its own is not very impressive; however, when you add them up, you just doubled your profit! In this particular diagram, you earned an extra $1,393 for free. You never had an extra visitor and you never did any extra work (except the time you took to set up this funnel).

Also note that this was just at 1,000 visitors; that' s a very low and easy number. Profit Academy students are consistently achieving 10,000 or more visitors a week! At those numbers, the double profits sales funnel would be earning you an extra $13,930 a week just thanks to this simple upsell/downsell process. That is huge!

Now that you're fully convinced, let's keep pushing forward and dive in even deeper. It's time you start getting awesome ideas on just how to build your own sales funnel.

A sales funnel (during the DPF stage) is comprised of only two elements that are easy to master:

- Upsells
- Downsells

In the next part of this chapter, I am going to make you a complete pro on just how to use upsells and downsells in your business.

Upsells

Upsells are simple. During the time that your customer is still in your shopping cart, any product that you offer is considered an upsell. When you buy your computer at the local electronics store and they offer you an extended warranty, they are "upselling" you.

Let's use an example.

We'll assume that you are selling a product that teaches people how to invest in the stock market. Your main product is $97 and it's a written and audio course that teaches your three specific secrets that allow you to make millions in the stock market.

Now, it's time to think of an upsell.

You have a few options when you're thinking of upsells. If you stick to any of these, you can come up with excellent ideas for almost any product you want.

Fast Options To Create Upsells

Remember, there are unlimited options and ways to create an upsell that is valuable; the following is just a small example to help your creative juices flow!

1. Advanced Material

Advanced material is one of the easiest ways to create an upsell. Using the stock-investing example, perhaps in your course, one of the three secrets is the most important. Also, you figure that this one secret is so great that it deserves its own course if someone really wants to master it.

You could simply create an additional, more detailed and advanced course on just that one strategy. In this case, say your main course is 300 pages, and you are covering the entire topic of stock investing. Your upsell course might also be 300 pages, but this time it will be all about that single secret.

This strategy is fast, simple, and converts very well for customers who just bought your course.

2. Different Form of Media

Many times people chose to use written or audio media as their main product. If this is the case, then you have an extremely easy upsell basically half done for you already. In our example of an investing course, assuming the course is written and audio, our author could simply take the same content and make a video course as well.

Perhaps being on video will allow the author to get into a bit more advanced techniques as well. However, mostly, video carries much higher value. Many times, students find it easier to learn with video so they are willing to pay more for it.

I have had a lot of students in the Profit Academy program choose this option and they are doing very well!

3. LIVE Training or Coaching Series

Talk about perceived value. Using "LIVE Training" is one of my absolute favorite forms of upsells. When I say "LIVE," I do not mean having to be on a stage with people sitting in front of you. That is too much work!

Again, thanks to the Internet, there are very simple automated technologies that allow you to run a *webinar conference*. All you need is a PowerPoint presentation, some notes, and you can run LIVE virtual teaching sessions.

In our example, you could create a six-week "boot camp" where you will personally get on a webinar with a small group of customers. You would then delve into each strategy in your course and personally teach, get more advanced, and even conduct a question-and-answer session.

When you offer LIVE training or coaching, you can easily raise the price into the hundreds and no one will blink an eye!

One more awesome tip is that you only have to do this six-week boot camp once. You can build the upsell product as you go, meaning that each week, you will add more content. Once you have taught your first group of students, during the first six weeks, you can just take the recordings and put them into the members area!

Perfect. You get the added perceived value of a LIVE training (with you) upsell. You can build it as you go (saving you a lot of time to launch). On top of that, you never have to repeat it; you can just record it once and you'll be done for the life of that sales funnel!

You can start to see now why I absolutely love using this upsell idea.

4. Software

Software programs are truly some of the best upsells. I don't personally use them too much because I am not a technical person. I don't like the thought of getting software developed. I have always been known as the "education guy." I like selling content and information.

However, the few times that having a software upsell made a lot of sense in my business, I did try it. The results were amazing. There is no better sales pitch than to tell a new customer, "Hey, you are about to learn exactly how to invest in the stock market using my three hidden secrets, but if you're in a rush, why not just skip the learning and let my software do it all for you, in just a few clicks."

Read that pitch again. Heck, even I'm sold!

Software can sell very well. The key is that you have to have software at your disposal and that it has to fit your market. For example, if you are in the market of teaching men how to talk to women, software might not be appropriate!

5. Horizontal Expansion

Here is your savior. In case the other four ideas just don't spark anything for you, you can use horizontal expansion.

Horizontal expansion is when you decide not to go more advanced or deeper in the same topic that you just sold your customer; rather, you decided to offer another new complimentary topic.

Let's go back to our example.

If your main product is about how to invest in the stock market, your upsell could be an entire course on how to use mutual funds to safely build long-term wealth. You see what I did there?

We did not position an upsell around the stock-investing topic. We added a new topic: mutual fund investing. This topic is highly complimentary. Obviously, anyone interested in stock investing would also have an interest in mutual fund investing. By doing this, you are simply going to repeat the steps in Section 3 and create yourself another product!

Easy, peasy.

Downsells

Downsells could not be easier!

There are really only two approaches to a downsell. Both approaches require your making almost no change to the actual upsell product. So, what exactly is a downsell?

A downsell comes up when you present an upsell offer to your customer. The customer declines. Almost 95% of the time, you will find that the customer declined the offer because he did not want to spend more money, or most likely he felt that it was too much.

This is when we deploy the downsell. A downsell is a final attempt to change that customer's mind by addressing his main concern: price. For years now, I use a standard rule with downsells. I reduce the price by 50%. If the upsell is $97, then the downsell becomes $47. If the upsell is $47, it becomes $27. As you can see, it is not exactly 50%, but close enough.

You get the idea.

Combining a major price decrease with the possibility that this will be his last chance to ever get this product usually does the trick.

You do not need to re-create a new product. Actually, you are still selling the same upsell product, with just a few tweaks.

- Remove some of the bonuses. Assuming you had added three to five bonuses to convince your customer to buy the upsell, you could remove a couple of these from the offer and justify cutting the price by 50%!

- Don't change the product at all. Just give a one-time only, last opportunity at 50% off. Now, some marketers feel this is wrong to their original customers who paid the full price for the upsell; some don't. Personally, I like to remove a few bonuses and make sure the price drop is justified. But, you can do either and be fine.

You have one more option in case you do not want to do a 50% discount or in case you do not want to remove any bonuses. You can add a payment plan. I have been deploying this strategy more and more lately for my more expensive upsells and it has worked very well!

Assuming you have a $247 upsell, you could offer the customer three payments of $97 each. This way, the perceived price (what he has to pay instantly) has been cut by even more than 50%; however, you have to make no changes and the downsell is more than justified.

Believe it or not, that's it. Downsells are so simple; there really is nothing more to it!

So, there you have it. The double profits formula really is that easy. This is exactly why so many of our Profit Academy students are able to fully implement it in a matter of days. However, it can very realistically double your profits and the profits that your affiliates make.

Of course, the more profits you make, the more you can invest in getting more traffic and hence feed the Circle of Profit!

Let's continue with the 5X Profit Secrets model. It is now time to teach you a strategy I call the **Backend Multiplier**. This is going to be your secret weapon in achieving $1 million. The backend multiplier is the final step to completing the Circle of Profit!

Chapter 23
Backend Multiplier – The Final Frontier to Your $1 Million

Imagine this: You've bought a new home. There were obviously tons of "options" you had when buying the house—all options that seemed to raise the price. Two weeks after you move in, your home builder sends you a letter offering you free interior-design services. You think to yourself, "Wow, just what I need and it's free!" You take him up on it.

Obviously, once the interior designer reaches your house, he will be making suggestions on what furniture and accessories to buy. Even more obviously, he will recommend you to a few select retailers. The truth is that the home builder will be making a commission from all the purchases you make.

The interior designer's compensation for the services comes from the stores. This sounds suspiciously like *affiliate marketing*, doesn't it? Keep this example in mind.

Let's envision another picture:

I recently purchased a Mac Pro from Apple. I noticed that within days of purchasing the Mac Pro, I began receiving from Apple telling me about how amazing their Cinema Display is. Suddenly, I started receiving stronger emails making me an offer to buy the product; not just one, but more than one (after all, my Mac Pro can support up to 6). Each of these is $997.

If you come to my office today, you will see three of them sitting there. Apple was able to turn my $3,000 purchase (the Mac Pro) into a $6,000 purchase (by adding three more Cinema Displays). Had Apple not spent time educating me specifically on the value of the Cinema Display, I would have bought much less expensive monitors else where.

Now, this sounds much like an upsell. However, it happened after I had left the store.

This brings us to what the *backend multiplier* is.

A backend multiplier is anything that you sell or endorse to your customer after she has left your shopping cart. In the terms of the Internet, this could be a day later, or my personal favorite, two weeks later.

There are two types of backend multipliers.

1. High Ticket Affiliate Offer. This is when you simply endorse a higher ticket ($497+) offer from someone else. You run a campaign promoting their product only to your customers, usually 10-14 days after they have become customers.

2. High Ticket Upsell. This is when you create your own product, training, coaching, mastermind, live event or workshop. Whatever you create, it's going to carry immense value and be something you market for $497.

I do incredibly well with both of these. That means, I use them both. I like to start with my own high ticket upsell first (because I do not have to share affiliate commissions with anyone) and then I do the high ticket affiliate offer. It's important that you note here the term *high ticket* is making its appearance over and over.

If you want to make the more profit, it is very important that your backend multiplier be focused on a $497 or higher price point. Considering that you are marketing to individuals who have proven to be buyers (as they have bought your product), you will make a lot more money by making a higher ticket offer.

Also, here is what really helps your profits go up because this transaction is happening weeks after the customer joined your company. Because it is only being marketed to your customers, you never have any affiliate commissions to pay! Imagine that.

You DOUBLE your margins right there. On all other sales you received during the cart, you had to pay at least 50% in commissions. Well, not on your backend multiplier.

Let's go back to an example we had used before. Remember Sammy, the Profit Academy student who was about to just "forget" the brilliant backend strategy and push forward with only her passion product (because she was eager and not patient)?

Sammy was able to create an extra $11,400 in pure profit simply by using both a high ticket affiliate offer and also her own high ticket offer. What this involved was Sammy doing promotions to her existing customers within the first month of the customer's joining.

The process of creating your high ticket offers is nothing different from what we discussed in Section #2; however, you just get more intimate and more advanced.

Chapter 24
Putting It All Together

As you can see, from the first day that you get your first subscriber to the day you create your backend multiplier, it's all a part of the same circle. If you want to turn your passion into $1 million, you're going to need to master each of these steps. I've spent over 10 years mastering this system and have trained thousands of students.

The reason I decided to create the Profit Academy program is specifically because there are too many talented people in this world who are miserable in their lives. I firmly believe that your talents, passions, hobbies, and expertise are gifts that you need to share with the world.

You never need to share without being able to also create full financial freedom for yourself.

Inside the Profit Academy program, we have a full team of coaches and a very strategic training schedule. We will take you from where you are today to where you dream of being, in a matter of just a few weeks. The main advice I always give to my students is that the entire process is just a series of steps. The key will be to follow our steps exactly.

No matter where you are and what step you are on, we've seen it all and we're prepared to hold you by the hand! The only catch is that I don't believe everyone is qualified to join the Academy. We do a very good job making sure that the entire class is full of only those students who are truly ready to dedicate themselves and change their lives.

If you want to see whether you qualify, please make sure to watch our additional training. All you need to do is go to www.FreeProfitWorkshop.com and register to attend our free training. It's important that I tell you that this workshop is completely free and there is no catch. The best part is that by attending this free workshop, you'll know very quickly whether the world of an online business is right for you.

During this free training, I will personally help you make the decision that is best for you and no one else.

If you are intrigued and want to start building your business, your next best step is to move into our Profit Workshop training and then qualify yourself to join the Profit Academy program.

What you have seen in this book so far is just a fraction of the whole picture. The amount of hand-holding and step-by-step coaching that we offer you is like nothing you have ever seen before! To get you to the next level, it will take some more training that is visual. I want to get in front of a white board and actually show you LIVE examples as well.

Through these four sections, you've gotten a good idea on what it takes to turn your passion into $1 million and how simple it can be.

In the next section, I want to go over what your exact next steps are. I also want to tell you where to get absolutely free training on how you market your new passion products.

What if you could generate that $1 million within the next 4 to 6 months?

Well, let me show you how to do that!

Section 5

Your Final Steps to $1 Million

Chapter 25
How to Generate $1 Million in Less Than Six Months

"Many of life's failures are people who did not realize how close they were to success when they gave up." – Thomas Edison

We've been through quite the journey together. I want to take some time to summarize it all. There is also one last missing piece. This is the piece that allows you to enter any niche on the Internet and create $1 million within six months or less. Of course, everyone works at his or her own pace; however, if you follow the system exactly (step-by-step), a million dollars in six months has been achieved many times!

The bulk of your time is in just creating excellent and valuable products that make up your funnel. You can choose to make those products yourself or you can outsource the entire process for pennies on the dollar.

The beauty of the Circle of Profit is that there is no one perfect way of using it. It's a very flexible system. You can tweak it to your own preferences as you wish. This section is just about that.

We are going to review each of the parts of the circle. I'll give you an estimated timeline (so you know just what to expect) and then finally, I'll give you the six-month plan that I've personally used multiple times to create $1 million over and over.

All right, it's time to go through what we learned and let me summarize it using the fastest tips and tricks for each part for the Circle.

Let's start right at the beginning.

Phase 1 – Building Your Audience: Starting to Profit

Phase 1 is quick to start and very simple. The main goal of this phase is to simply choose your niche and start building a subscriber list. You then use automated technology to send valuable content to this list via email. You can start this phase in less than one hour a day.

The goal of this phase to get you to start building subscribers so when you decide to launch into Phase 2, you'll have an existing group of buyers ready!

1. Traffic

Reasonable Time to Expect: Starts within 24 Hours

For any business on the Internet, you need people to visit your website. We've created a simple click-by-click system that you can copy and paste. As long as you follow a few steps, you will have more traffic than you know what to do with!

Also, each niche (or topic) is different. Different traffic sources will work better in some niches than others. In our Academy, we are full of world-class experts who specialize in any form of traffic you can imagine. This means that you also become a master in it all:

- Email Media
- Google
- Facebook
- Bing
- Yahoo
- Display Advertising
- Social Media
- Forum Marketing
- Search Engine Optimization
- *And so many more!*

Get ready to master all these sources of traffic, all from just one training academy!

2. Opt-In Page

Reasonable Time to Expect: Maximum Three Days to Build (even less with our technology)

This is the quickest way to capture subscribers. An opt-in page is the highest converting page of all types on the Internet. It's the easiest to make (we even have simple technology you can use).

This page makes a free offer in order to get your site visitors to give you their email address.

You can start making hundreds of thousands of dollars on line by having only a one-page website: an opt-in page!

3. Autoresponders and Broadcasting

Reasonable Time to Expect: Two to Three Days to Fully Set Up, Then 20-30 Minutes a Day After That.

As you build subscribers, you're going to begin communicating with them. That is exactly what we use autoresponders and broadcasting for. You can log into one central place, type one email, and it will automatically go out to all your subscribers!

We discussed the many kinds of autoresponders that are in the market and exactly which one you should use (and how I have my own service now that I can get you free for 90 days). We also went through the detailed styles of emails that you should write to your subscribers. As you join the Academy, we will even provide you with actual templates!

That wraps up Phase 1! Quick, isn't it? However, it's a very important phase and we have some incredible tricks to make it 10 times easier and faster. Also, the real profits and financial freedom lie in Phase 2. Let's keep rolling forward!

Phase 2 – Rolling Your Way to $1 Million

4. Passion Product

Reasonable Time to Expect: From Planning to Completion, Three to Four Weeks

After you've confirmed that you have chosen the right profitable passion product, you follow a simple series of steps to create a highly valuable training product. This product will be your presence on the Internet. You will begin to easily market this product and instantly double the profits you are making from Phase 1.

Your passion product can be either written, audio, video, or a mix of all three. You can easily master the production of all three media. They require a small budget and normal household tools to create.

Even better, we teach you precisely how to outsource the entire process if you want.

5. Double Profits Formula

Reasonable Time to Expect: From Planning to Completion, Two to Three Weeks

Ideally, you will create the products needed for the double profits formula at the same time as you are creating your passion product. The double profits formula requires at least two additional products (with additional bonuses) that are placed in your *shopping cart funnel*.

This means as soon as the customer purchases your passion product and before gaining access to that product, you will offer at least one or two opportunities to upgrade the order (invest more money in your advanced training).

It is consistently proven that this one strategy alone will double your profits. If you were making $100 per customer, you will instantly start making $200. If done using your system, it should never take you more than three to four weeks (and you can build this as you are building your passion product).

6. Backend Multiplier

Reasonable Time to Expect: From Planning to Completion, One to Two Weeks

A major profit-generating strategy that many online businesses miss out on is what I call the *backend multiplier*. This is the part where you position a high-ticket offer, $497 or higher, to your customer starting one to two weeks after she or he becomes a customer.

There are two kinds of high-ticket offers I almost always promote to my customers:

1. My Own High-Ticket Offer
2. An Affiliate High-Ticket Offer

I will typically create a more intimate training program with more access to me or to my top trainers and price it at $497 or above. This offer seriously helps boost my profit margins considering I do not have to pay affiliate commissions on it!

Following my own high-ticket offer (about two weeks after that) I will position a high-ticket affiliate offer. This means the entire offer is owned by someone else and I am simply promoting it as an affiliate. Given the higher price, I make large commissions without adding any work to my plate.

All of these strategies together give me a 500% boost in my profits, which allows me to scale my business much faster!

7. Profits

Reasonable Time to Expect: Within One Week of Phase 1 Launch

Profits are, of course, what this entire business is about! You should start seeing some level of profits very early in the process with just your email list. The major jump in profits will come once you start creating your own products and funnels.

Remember, the more profit you make, you have to re-invest a portion every month, religiously, back into your business. Use those funds to invest in more traffic, more training, more products, all of it. The more you follow our system to invest your profits in the right places, the easier you will fly past our $1 million goal

There you have it.

That's the Circle of Profit, as simple as can be, yet completely revolutionary. I want you to keep learning and join me farther and deeper. The more we work together, you will learn some amazing shortcuts and secrets that make each step far easier and 10 times faster.

This is just the beginning of our journey together. I've invested 10 years of my life into this program, and all I ask is that you go through it all, one step at a time.

Chapter 26
Quick Checklists – Keeping Yourself Organized

As you get ready to start your passion business, the following list is going to be very helpful. Remember, if you're serious, you need to continue your training. We can actually help guide you the entire way. You can even get a hands-on coach and mentors (who have done it themselves) to guide you.

Phase 1: Building Your Audience

- Choose Niche (*Passion + Many Affiliate Offers to Promote*)
- Create Free Giveaway
- Opt-in Page
- Sign Up for Autoresponder (*We Give 90 Days Free for Profit Academy Students at SendLane.com*)
- Write 10-Day Autoresponder Sequence
- Choose TYP Affiliate Offer
- Start Generating Traffic (*Investment Traffic and/or Free Traffic*)

Phase 2: Launching Your Passion Product

- Confirm Niche (*Use Specific Formula Taught to Assure Profitability*)
- Research Top 5-10 Products in Same Niche/Topic
- Create Product Outline
- Create Product (*or have it outsourced*)
- Sales Material - Written or Video (*Taught in Great Detail Inside Profit Academy; Template Samples Provided as Well*)
- Decide on Double Profits Formula Sales Funnel
  - Upsell #1

- - Downsell #1
- - Upsell #2
- - Downsell #2
- ○ Decide on Backend Multiplier
- - High-Ticket Offer
- - Affiliate High-Ticket Offer
- ○ Create Products For Brilliant Backend (*Above*)
- ○ Test Entire Funnel (*More on This Below*)

As you can see, if you're truly dedicated, it doesn't have to take long at all before you can turn your passions into great profits. All you need to do is follow the Circle of Profit and the simple steps that our system gives you (if you're ready to start right away).

I encourage you to go back and read this book again and also to watch all the free training we provide for you here: www.FreeProfitWorkshop.com. You will be amazed at how simple I will make the process for you!

CASE STUDY: My Personal $1 Million Snowball Launch
How I Created My Offer: Future of Wealth

Back in 2004, when I started learning online marketing. I was never meant to become an expert in entrepreneurism or online marketing. I always wanted to be in the personal-development niche; that is my main passion. However, I started getting so good at online marketing and attracting so many students that eight years later, it was still my main business.

However, in 2012, when I was seeing my worst days in business, I made myself a promise:

"When I climb out of these dark days, I will publish my first product on just how I did it. I will teach the world all the mind-strategies I have used to save my life and save my wealth."

In early 2013, I had done it. It was time to make good on my own promise.

I sat down and in one night I went through the entire outline. It was almost as if the entire course was just pouring out of me! After that, I never hired an outsourcer, not for this product. Instead, I called one of my best friends, he brought his camera and lights, and we set up a video studio.

I was actually living in India at this time and so we shot the entire course right in my apartment there. We used flipcams; these were literally $100 cameras and we created a product that has gone on to sell millions of dollars worth!

The entire outline and product creation took me less than two weeks. I was on fire!

As I finished my main product, I sat down to review the outline and evaluate what I felt was missing. What else could I add to the product to make it even better? Based on what I discovered, I created more outlines. I was outlining additional upsells for my funnel and also some bonuses to give away for Free.

Again, between using my computer's microphone and a $100 camera, I was back to creating the remainder of the products for my funnel.

In less than 30 days, I had achieved a lifelong dream. My first entire personal development product was complete and it was amazing. I was very impressed and very proud of what I had created. I knew, for sure, that I would be changing lives.

But there was a big problem now.

I didn't know anything about how to market in this niche. I imagine you must be thinking the same thing right now, right? "Anik, I can create the product, fine, but how will I sell it?"

Well, even though I'd had eight years of marketing experience, I didn't know a single person in the personal-development arena. It was as if I was starting from the very beginning. So, I turned to the very system I teach in the Profit Academy program!

I built my funnel and it was time for the **snowball launch** (next chapter).

Now, we have spent great time discussing the "mechanics" of what you need in order to turn your passion into $1 million. There is just one main topic left: How exactly do you launch this new product (and brilliant backend sales funnel) to the market. How do you turn your amazing new products into easy profits?

That's next.

Chapter 27
The Snowball Launch – Rolling Your Way to $1 Million

I call it the *snowball launch*. In the Free Profit Workshop, I spend the entire third training session discussing the snowball launch. To best understand how this amazing strategy works, you really need to see me in front of a white board. Nonetheless, I'm going to introduce you to it here!

The snowball launch can be broken down into its own three phases:

1. Testing
2. Power of One
3. Official Announcement

These three phases can take as long as you want; however, if you follow our system exactly, each of them should be relatively short.

I'll introduce you to each one.

1. Testing

Assuming you have finished your passion product, your sales funnel, and have everything ready to go, it's time to test the process. When you test your process, you are testing for two main things:

- Technically: Does it work?
- Sales Conversions: Is it converting well?

We have not discussed the simple technology aspects yet. However, I get into great detail on just how to actually make all the nuts and bolts work. I will walk you through how to easily accept money online and create your own members areas. I even show you how to create great sales pages without ever knowing a line of HTML!

Before you can ever start aggressively getting traffic, you will want to do a test order and make sure everything is working. As long as your processes are working "technically," it will be time to test your sales conversions.

Testing requires you to get a slight amount of investment traffic. You can test with as little as $300. The key to remember is that if you have followed our instructions exactly, you are not really risking any money. You will earn that money back very fast. With your own products, the good news is that you are making 100% of the margin. You are also getting a lifetime customer. Any traffic you invest in for testing is very safe.

Having said that, I still always recommend you start slowly and scale.

CASE STUDY: My Personal $1 Million Snowball Launch
How I Tested a New Offer

You will soon see a case study below where I created $1 million in less than six months in a brand-new niche. However, it all began at testing. What exactly did I do test this offer?

The product I created is called **Future of Wealth** and it teaches you specific wealth mindset strategies that allow the law of attraction to work in your life. We are 100% focused on wealth generation in this course.

I spent exactly six weeks creating the entire product funnel. However, during that six weeks, I was also building profit by building my own email list!

When it came time to launch my product, I had to first test it.

#1 – First, I sent an Email to my own list. This will always lead to better conversions than any other form of marketing. If your numbers are bad even on this traffic, then you need to rework your sales material.

#2 – I invested $500 in email media. I was able to immediately make $600. I was able to profit on my test traffic! The key was that I followed this Profit Academy system exactly; it eliminates almost any risk you have.

#3 – Next, I invested $1,000 in email media. Again, I recovered by generating $1,500 within the first 24 hours. I continued to improve my processes with all the data I was collecting.

#4 – I invested $500 in Facebook traffic. Here, I was able to generate $750. Again, I profited. My numbers were looking great and I knew I was ready to take it to the next step; it was time for the "Power of One" to kick in!

All of my students have used a very similar model to test their new offers and it has never once failed them.

You never want to start scaling your traffic before testing and having as much data as possible. You especially never want to use the "Power of One" strategy until you are at least 90% sure that your entire funnel is converting very well. The main thing you want to ensure is that the funnel is converting well enough for your affiliates. If you were to promote your own product as an affiliate, would your commissions lead you to getting as close to $1 per click earnings?

2. Power of One

The power of one might be one of the greatest marketing tools you ever have in your business. This one strategy alone has saved my life many times.

- It helped start my business in 2005.
- It helped grow my business to $10 million in 2008.
- It helped save my business in 2012.
- It helped me launch into my true passion niche in 2013.
- It helped me build an empire training for entrepreneurs in 2014.

The best part is that my students are using the Power of One every single day with just as much (if not more) success than I!

From a $300/Month Salary to $1 Million
Student: Ritoban C.

I want to tell you a story of a student who has now become one of my closest friends. He sent me an email one day from India. Now, I get a lot of emails like this and unfortunately cannot respond to them all. However, something in his email made me stop in my tracks.

I noticed he was from the same city that my family grew up in. It's a small city in India. I had never met any marketer or student from there! I got excited and responded.

He wanted to learn how to release his own product on the Internet. You see, he used to have a job, just like everyone, he was making $300 a month. In India, that is about what any new graduate generates as a full-time income. He wanted more for himself, though.

He spent night and day studying online marketing, and he was able to use affiliate marketing to get himself past making $10,000 a month! He quit his job. But he still wanted more! That was why he sent me an email. He said he wanted to go to the next level.

For the next thirty to forty-five days, all I did was put him through the same Profit Academy system. Within just 60 days of his sending me an email, he had generated his first $1 million on the Internet.

His life has never been the same; I'll tell you his story in more detail in the next chapter. That day, when he first emailed me, he didn't know it, but I personally became his Power of One.

For him (as with hundreds of my students), the Power of One has been the greatest contributor to that $1 million goal!

The Power of One proves and says that you need to have only ONE good contact or affiliate in any niche and you can take it over. Even if you are entering into a niche and don't know anyone, I'm going to show you how to find at least one person that will respond to your email (just like I did for Ritoban). It isn't hard; seriously, it's just a numbers game!

If you use my system exactly to send out at least 10 emails or Skype chats, I will bet my left pinky that at least one person will respond to you. That's it. Congratulations. If you nurture that one relationship the way I teach you, and you are going to be well on your way to your first $1 million.

The way that the Power of One works is that just one person is enough to create a viral network for you. This one person will be able to test promoting your product as an affiliate. This person will become a friend. You will take great care of that One. You will make sure that when the One promotes your product, the One gets excellent results and conversions.

Remember, an affiliate is someone who will send you traffic and you will, in turn, give that person a commission (50-75%). The person promoting for you will always want to get as close to making $1 a click in commissions. If you can get close or past that number, you are golden. By the way, this is why I preach about testing an offer first. You want to make sure before going into this Power of One relationship that you have no risk on the table!

Here's how the viral element begins.

As soon as this person finishes promoting your product, you take her results and report the results back to her. Assuming the results are stellar and this person is happy with them, you simple ask her to introduce you to at least three other friends on Skype or email. Remember, if someone has been in this niche for some time, she will know a lot of other people just like herself!

Why Phase 1 Is Key for Your Power of One

Let's talk about that last part of the Circle that we have not mentioned yet. You see the **reciprocation** line that comes back to becoming traffic for you. This is a very key line if you want to generate $1 million!

Remember, during Phase 1 you have been promoting the products of others to generate your revenue. One of the best ways (if not the absolute best way) to find the one best person to start your networking with is to contact the very person you have been promoting through Phase 1 the entire time.

Money talks!

This person is at least 1,000% more likely to respond to you because he feels indebted to you. You've already made him a lot of money!

The Power of One is one of the main reasons I preach that Phase 1 is so important. You generate profits during Phase 1, and you also get a chance to build some great relationships. These relationships will be a godsend for you when it comes time to release your own products.

I have seen my students use the Power of One in many niches. From Internet marketing, investing, to personal development and even the dating market; I've witnessed the Power of One launch massive businesses that tower past $1 million!

Inside the Profit Academy system, I will give you my best strategies to build your network using the Power of One. Even if you are extremely shy, I will show you just what to do!

CASE STUDY: My Personal $1 Million Snowball Launch
How The Power of One Started Everything For Me

* * *

I had the product. I had the funnel. I had even tested my offer.

Now, I needed to make some major moves. I needed to get to $1 million as fast as possible. Well, I decided to use the Power of One. The difference is that I decided to use it three times, not just once!

Power of One #1:

In order to test my funnel, I had been buying email media from three different marketers. This means I was consistently buying personal-development clicks from them to market my product. In the process of doing this, I began to have a lot of conversations with the sellers.

We used to chat on Skype and all three became friends with me. They also saw me consistently buying advertising for my product and wanted to know more information about how it was converting.

In the process of talking to them, they started to refer me to their friends. I asked them to help me find affiliates who would help me launch the product. Not one of them said no; they went off introducing me to everyone they could!

Power of One #2:

Before I finished created my **Future of Wealth** product, I had been practicing Phase 1 and had built up an email list of nearly 10,000 subscribers. During this time there was one particular offer I promoted very aggressively. I was making most of my income using this one affiliate offer.

I had made the owner of the offer thousands of dollars as well!

I reached out to him and in less than eight hours we were talking on Skype and he had already connected me to five of his top affiliates. Wow!

* * *

Power of One #3:

Using one of the connections I had made from my previous Power of One, I got invited to a small personal-development LIVE event. I hopped on the plane and spent three days with some of the top marketers in personal development. Of course, there was no better place to meet people. However, I focused all my energies on one of the main marketers there.

He and I went out to lunch together and really hit it off. He pledged his support. He told me he would make sure I met everyone in the space. I didn't know if I should believe him, but I was excited.

Surely enough, just seven days later, he sent out more than 65 personal-introduction emails. The contacts I made from his introductions have gone on to make me millions of dollars since that day.

This was all because of the Power of One. As you join my system, I will make sure you are a master at it!

Remember, you can be shy. You can be an introvert. It doesn't matter. The Power of One can be fully done behind your computer, using nothing but digital tools. I will walk you through the entire system in so much detail, you won't even know when you master it and start to profit from it!

3. Official Announcement

One you give the Power of One a few weeks to accumulate, your network grows, and you have fully tested your funnel, you will officially announce your launch. At this point, you are going to aggressively seek other affiliates who will send you traffic in exchange for a commission.

Putting together a product launch is an art in and of itself. The process of doing this reaches outside the scope of this book. However, our students are taught every detail of the process and have gone on to create massive results!

Actually, if you use the Power of One correctly, the official announcement will start itself. The main part of the official announcement is for you to pick a period of time and throw in some prizes for the affiliates.

Perhaps you declare a window of three weeks and convince your affiliates to promote during that window. In exchange, you are running a contest. You give away cool prizes to your affiliates for their support. You will be shocked at how differently affiliates will react to your contact when you give them a designated period of time in which they need to send their email.

They key is to just make sure that you have fully tested the offer and are happy with the results!

CASE STUDY: My Personal $1 Million Snowball Launch
The Final Key to My $1 Million Launch

I used the Power of One to have at least ten different affiliates promote my product for me. They all had excellent results. These affiliates were actually excited to go out and promote my product to other affiliates. They were happy to connect me to anyone I asked for.

At this point, I chose a window that was one month long. (I chose a longer window so I could give myself more time to meet all my new contacts.) During this window, I put together a superb list of prizes and a contest.

The affiliates are all friends with each other, but they are also very competitive.

Going into the official product launch, I had nearly 1,000 sales for my product (through my testing campaigns and also through the ten affiliates who had helped me test by promoting). However, by the time my one-month launch was over, I had over 10,000 sales.

That is the kind of power a good product launch can bring to your income. I had surpassed my $1 million goal with flying colors during that one-month period. The best part is that the entire funnel and everything was already done. During that one-month period, I never did anything other than simply contact affiliates.

Every affiliate I contacted was through the Internet. Every affiliate I contacted was easily introduced to me by a friend. I never cold-called or "sold" anyone. Because of the warm introduction, almost every person I met was very welcoming.

I had gone from not knowing anyone in the entire personal-development niche to knowing almost everyone. I did it all using Skype and Facebook. I did it in less than 60 days.

I would never turn back after that. Since that day, I have consistently generated more than $1 million in every product I release. I have a long list of great friendships and affiliates to rely on for any product I release.

I should also add that because of all the traffic these affiliates sent me, my Phase 1 income went through the roof. I built an email list of over 100,000 subscribers and have since been able to rely on more than $1 million a year in affiliate income. This is on top of the income I make from my own products!

This is why I call it the Circle of Profit. Once it starts feeding itself, it never stops.

The snowball launch is so important that I have dedicated an entire training session on our Profit Workshop just for it. If you want to see just how we release your new passion product and funnel to world, please make sure to watch Training #3 of our Free Profit Workshop (*www.FreeProfitWorkshop.com*).

Remember, you get completely free access to this workshop because you have shown the initiative by reading this book. It's my gift to you! Make sure to go register for it and you will also be able to learn more about whether you qualify to join us inside the Profit Academy!

Chapter 28

The $15 Million Student

A Message From One of My Top Students

When one of my top students found out I'm writing this book, he insisted on writing a message for you. Of all the students I've ever had, his results are the most inspiring. The only difference between him and my other students is that I've rarely seen the kind of determination he has shown.

He works hard. He lives his life to the fullest. He fights for his dreams. Mostly, he really puts the Circle of Profit into full use. He fuels the Circle every single day. The amazing thing is that he is also one of my best friends.

He started using the exact system behind the Profit Academy a little over three years ago. The results he has achieved are absolutely awe-inspiring. In 2015, he's well on his way to generating over $15 million in sales online (and probably over $4 Million in profit). I consistently joke with him now and have named him "The $15 Million Man."

In the Words of Jimmy Kim

"You have to believe in yourself and you have to take action; anybody can do this."

I used to work very hard. I'm talking over 16-hour days. I started my career washing cars at a dealership. I showed a lot of dedication and in just a few years, I worked my way up to the top management in the same dealership! As great as that was, it also meant waking up by 6:00 a.m. and not getting back home until 11:00 p.m.

* * *

Even when I made good money, I barely had time to enjoy it. I did this for years and years and I couldn't take it anymore. I was so exhausted and the thought of doing that for the rest of my life made me stay up all night.

That was when I came across Anik and his training. Honestly, I never believed it initially. I thought it was all fake and a lie. How can someone make millions of dollars just sitting at home. If this was really possible, why wasn't everyone doing it?

I lived in doubt for quite some time. Then, one day, I just couldn't take the day to day grind any more and I decided to go out on a limb and try what Anik was talking about. I have to tell you, I was immediately hooked.

Not only did it work, it worked fast!

Within the first 30 days, I was in profit. Within the first 60 days, I was making the same income I had made in my full-time management job. Now, understand this. I had taken over six years to get into my management job. Here, I was able to get to the same income in just two months. Imagine: six years versus two months.

That was it. From there, I never looked back.

My first year as an online entrepreneur following the Profit Academy system, I was able to generate over $250,000. The problem is, I was still being a bit lazy. I never released my own product. I generated $250,000 by only using Phase 1.

Then, my second year, I decided to treat my business like a true business and get serious. I got involved with product development and my income that year jumped straight to $1 million. This is profit, by the way; that is what I actually earned.

My third year, I continued to grow. I entered new niches; I released more products and made new partnerships using the Circle of Profit. I again doubled my income and made close to $2 million.

This year, I'm already on track to generate over $15 million in sales and easily create over $4 million in profit. I just bought my dream home in San Diego. I drive my dream cars. I really do live the life of my dreams.

People ask me all the time how I did this and I have to say, it's just the simple system that Anik taught me. That's it.

The only thing I added to the mix was my sheer dedication and belief. I had faith. I worked hard and I took action. I'm looking you in the eyes right now and telling you, "You can do this. This is real. Everything inside the Profit Academy is life-changing in ways you cannot even imagine."

The only thing you need:

"You have to believe in yourself and you have to <u>take action</u>."

Jimmy is one of our star students because he immediately went to work and worked hard. He always took action and has always been foot-first when there is an opportunity to learn. I will never say that $15 million is typical results. I would also never promise you any kind of results at all. That would not be fair.

However, I do want you to read his story and see all that is possible. He never, ever thought he would be an online entrepreneur. He did not even know this world exists. He came into it completely fresh. He simply took our system, put it into action, and worked at it until he started making millions.

Even to this day, as I type this, he's working the system. He understands that the more he fuels the Circle of Profit, the greater his profits will be!

Chapter 29
Our Student Who Escaped Iraq

Living the American Dream; It's Still Alive!

This next story is just incredible. Zane Baker started with Profit Academy in 2014 and has become an incredibly success in almost no time. What's even more amazing is Zane's story. If anyone ever saw him three years ago, no one would ever say that he would be an online Entrepreneur living the life of his dreams!

- Born and raised in Baghdad, Iraq
- English is his second language
- Zero experience in business
- No experience in online marketing
- Failed for three years trying online marketing!

Zane came to us as his last resort. He was ready to give up. He had been through so many other programs to try to learn that he was fed up. He just wasn't seeing any success.

Zane escaped Iraq a few years ago and settled down in America. He wanted nothing more than to live the American Dream and achieve financial freedom. Of course, to make ends meet, he found a job and started working day and night. Suddenly, he found himself spending hours in traffic, barely making enough money to make ends meet, and completely drained of his passion.

He wanted a lot more from life. He wanted to live a life of complete financial freedom. Well, some how he came across the world of online marketing. He was hooked. He immediately began to try. He went through every course he could find. He tried to hire coaches. Nothing was working.

One day, he came across the Profit Academy training program and he openly says now that his entire life changed. He went from not being able to make a dime on the Internet to quitting his day job!

Zane just recently had his first month where he earned $10,000. He was ecstatic and wanted to write the following letter for you.

Zane Baker

"The first feeling I had when I made my first $10,000…"

Growing up in Iraq, you can imagine the background I come from. I was raised in practically the slums of Iraq. I didn't know English. I didn't have any business experience or anything. After escaping to America, I did what everyone does: I got a job.

I always knew I wanted more for my life, but I didn't know where to turn. I barely knew anyone in the entire country, much less, anyone in business who could help me.

One day, I fell into the world of online marketing. I thought I had my answer, but as it turned out, I didn't. I spent two years and every penny of my savings trying to find a system that actually worked. Let me tell you, there are hundreds of systems that you can buy online, you have to be very careful.

Then, one day, I was scrolling the Internet and I came across Anik's programs. Something about him just felt right, I really felt that he was the real deal. I decided to take a leap of faith and give it a try. Looking back now, I'm so grateful that I had the right mind to do it. Had I missed that opportunity, I'd still be stuck in the morning traffic for two hours, even today.

I've followed the Profit Academy system exactly and have seen nothing but amazing results. I am growing every single month. My email list is now over 20,000 and growing by leaps and bounds every month. I'm also very proud to announce that I just crossed my first $10,000 month in January 2015!

The first feeling I had when I made my first $10,000 was of pure relief. I had done it! I was so excited I couldn't sit straight. I officially know now that the day when I am a multi-millionaire and completely free is just a reach away. It's just a matter of continuing to follow the system and I'm virtually guaranteed to make it!

The system really does work. It works just as Anik says it will. The only thing you need to do is take action. Period. Don't think. Don't question. As Nike says, "Just do it!"

Chapter 30
Your Exact Next Steps

First, let me start by congratulating you on how far you've come. You have to take a moment to really be proud of yourself because most never make it even this far. Everyone loves to talk about all the big things they want to do, but few have the true passion and desire to give it what it needs.

This book is just step one of the process to turning your passion into $1 million. If you'll allow me, I really want to be your head coach and lead you through the entire process.

There are two major next steps that will allow you to work together with me and my trainers much more closely.

Step #1 – Claim Your Free Profit Workshop Bonus ($1,497 Value)

Please immediately go to: www.FreeProfitWorkshop.com and register yourself right away! It's absolutely free and all it takes is an email to register. This Free Profit Workshop consists of three trainings where I will again walk you through the entire system, but this time you can see me visually doing every step!

- Watch and learn LIVE as I teach all the ins and outs of your own passion business.
- Meet our successful students and watch as I review their businesses with you.
- Have an opportunity to ask your questions.
- Join our community of passion business builders. Imagine being surrounded by thousands of people just like yourself!

You can get all of this for free.

Even if you have missed our LIVE presentations, I am going to make the replays available for a limited time only. The replays are also free and you can watch them at your own pace as well!

Training #1 – How To Make Your First $100,000
(LIVE on February 23ʳᵈ at 8:00 p.m. Eastern)

Training #2 – The 5X Multiplier – One Trick to
Immediately Turning Your Passion Into $500,000
(LIVE on February 26ᵗʰ at 8:00 p.m. Eastern)

Training #3 – The Snowball Launch – The Final Step to
Turning Your Passion Into $1 Million
(LIVE on March 2ⁿᵈ at 8:00 p.m. Eastern)

Mark Your Calendars: This Is Serious!

Listen, taking action is absolutely key. You will see no changes in your life unless you take these opportunities and seize them. The Free Profit Workshop is easily worth more than $1,497. Other marketers would never even release this information, much less sell it at $1,497. I want to hand it to you for free because I really want to empower you with whatever it takes to make your dreams come true.

Make sure to actually *mark your calendars*. Take this seriously. Be prepared to go through each of the training sessions with pen and paper for your notes. I have no idea when this will be done again, so take action now!

Beyond our Free Profit Workshop, there will be some of you who really want to add rockets to your business. For the students who truly want to see themselves achieve $1 million before the next four to six months are over, you're going to want to join our Profit Academy.

However, the Profit Academy program is very limited and we are only taking qualified students. The best way to know if you qualify is to actually attend the entire Profit Workshop. You will come to learn a lot more there!

Step #2 – Join Our Profit Community at the Profit Academy

($1,497 Value)

I've dreamed of putting together a community like this for years. I have actively spent the last 18 months preparing to release this community to the world. If you want to work fast and have a hands-on coach to guide you, you need to immediately join our Profit Academy.

- Step-by-Step Video Training
- Weekly Webinar Coaching
- Full Q&A Opportunities
- Profit Mentors, Working with You Around The Clock
- Technology + Software – Everything You Need To Launch and Manage Your Business
- Virtual Workshops – Take Weekend Workshops Right From Your
  Home, Become a Master at Every Topic Needed to Create $1 Million!
- LIVE Event in Vegas – Join Our Profit Students in Vegas for a LIVE Event, Network & Learn From Experts Around The World!
- LIVE Examples You Can Copy – We Build Out Entire Businesses That You Can Model Right After!

This is literally *just the beginning* of what we will do for you. My entire team is at your disposal. We are here if you are ready. The rest lies in your hands!

Your passion business waits around the corner for you. You can start building a life of true financial freedom starting today. All you need to do is officially declare it and then follow the entire Profit Academy system exactly.

That's it.

If you're ready, we are.

I want to wish you the very best in your business. I wish you millions in profit and a life full of nothing but your dreams coming true. If I can personally do anything to help you achieve that, you know where to find me.

Looking forward to our journey together!